CHILD WEL   OF AMERICA

NATIONAL BLUEPRINT

FOR EXCELLENCE IN CHILD WELFARE

STANDARDS OF EXCELLENCE:

Raising the Bar for Children,
Families, and Communities

CWLA Press is an imprint of the Child Welfare League of America. The Child Welfare League of America is the nation's oldest and largest membership-based child welfare organization. We are committed to engaging people everywhere in promoting the well-being of children, youth, and their families, and protecting every child from harm. All proceeds from the sale of this book support CWLA's programs in behalf of children and families.

CHILD WELFARE LEAGUE OF AMERICA, INC.
HEADQUARTERS
1726 M Street NW, Suite 500
Washington, DC 20036
www.cwla.org

CURRENT PRINTING (last digit)
10 9 8 7 6 5 4 3 2 1

Cover and text design by Marlene Saulsbury
Edited by Rachel Adams

Printed in the United States of America

ISBN: 978-1-58760-152-1

Library of Congress Cataloging-in-Publication

CONTENTS

FOREWORD

As a coalition of private and public entities and individuals dedicated to ensuring the safety, permanency, and well-being of children, youth, and their families, the Child Welfare League of America (CWLA) advocates for policies, best practices, and collaborative strategies that advance positive outcomes for children and youth.

Established as an outcome of the first White House Conference on the Care of Dependent Children in 1909, CWLA initially worked with the Children's Bureau and other stakeholders to end child labor, increase the number of children receiving critical immunizations, establish child care and homemaker services, and secure other improvements in the lives of children and families in the general population. Over the course of its history, CWLA increasingly turned its efforts to ensuring better outcomes for the children and families that are most vulnerable by working to address reported cases of abuse and neglect, quality and availability of services for children removed from their homes, family supports, and access to services for children in their communities.

In recent years, actualizing our mission has become ever more complex. It is clear that the needs of the most vulnerable cannot be addressed outside of the context of that which impacts all children and families in society. The reality is that many children in this country experience challenges because of issues with immigration, education, housing, and health care, or because they live in communities where there is violence and poverty. As an organization that has, as its core mission, working with the children and families that are most challenged, we see the most devastating outcomes of the failure of this country to do all it can for its children. Unless the community has what it needs and takes ownership for ensuring the well-being of all of its children and families, neither children and families who are vulnerable nor children and families in general will flourish. The National Blueprint returns CWLA to our historic roots of advocating for a multi-system, community-based approach to protecting children and supporting families. This approach is grounded in the practice improvement work that is specific to the child welfare system and inclusive of its advocacy efforts on behalf of all children, youth, and families.

A critical focus of our work will be to advance a child welfare system that is linked to and operates in partnership with families and communities. It is clear that traditional public and private child welfare organizations cannot be solely responsible for the well-being of children and families. While the child welfare system has a distinct set of responsibilities to care for children identified as at risk of abuse and neglect, it must do its work by sharing its knowledge and resources and leveraging the knowledge and resources gained from families, communities, and other systems—such as health, education, or juvenile justice—that can contribute to better outcomes for children and families. Too often, the needs of children, youth, and families are addressed by multiple systems that are not working together but rather in functional silos. A major focus of the CWLA National Blueprint is to help entities to improve cooperation, collaboration, and communication to diminish or eradicate these functional silos.

Through the National Blueprint, CWLA articulates the foundation and framework for achieving the vision *that all children will grow up safely, in loving families and supportive communities, with everything they need to flourish—and with connections to their culture, ethnicity, race, and language.* However, just as an architect's blueprint provides a plan but leaves many decisions to be made during construction, the CWLA National Blueprint does not pretend to either identify or address all of the necessary transition questions and answers. Many questions must be addressed to determine how to construct supports and services aligned with the CWLA National Blueprint. As each community, organization, family, and individual is unique, the obstacles to implementation will only be identified as people work together to achieve the National

Blueprint. This will require them to set priorities and make compromises along the way. These changes may not be easy, and will take time, but they should not hinder everyone from working collectively toward a society in which all children and youth can flourish.

Development of CWLA Standards of Excellence

Since the inception of its program of standards development, CWLA has formulated a series of standards based on current knowledge and children's developmental needs, and has tested ways of meeting these needs most effectively. The preparation of standards involves an examination of current practices and the assumptions on which they are based; a survey of the professional literature and standards; and a study of the most recent experiences of social work and related fields—child development, child care, education, mental health, psychology, medicine, psychiatry, and sociology—and other appropriate and pertinent fields such as management, business, technology, communication, and marketing, as they bear on child welfare practice and management.

The final formulation of standards follows an extended discussion of principles and issues by experts in each service area; the drafting of a preliminary statement; and a critical review by CWLA member agencies, representatives of related professions, and other national organizations.

CWLA's preparation of standards involves the wide participation of local, state, and national agency representatives. Many CWLA member agencies, including state human service departments and private agencies, have contributed the professional time and travel costs of their staff members who developed these standards, reviewed draft statements, and made suggestions for revision. Representatives from national organizations, governmental agencies, sectarian agencies, universities, and professional associations in related fields have taken part in the various committees.

To maintain their visionary quality, CWLA standards are subject to continual review and revision because knowledge about children, families, communities, human behavior, and the treatment of human needs continues to grow. Developments in management and the social sciences; the continuing evaluation of the effectiveness of current social service practices, policies, and programs; and shifting patterns of social values and social organizations all lead to the continued modification of the vision for quality in child welfare practice and management.

CWLA Standards from an International Perspective

CWLA standards are frequently requested by officials, child welfare professionals, and advocates from other countries who are interested in learning what is considered best practice in North America in a range of practice areas. Countries in Europe, Asia, the Middle East and the Americas have drawn from the CWLA standards to develop and improve services. The CWLA Standards of Excellence for Adoption Services also served as a reference for the development of the Hague Convention Regulations on Intercountry Adoption.

CWLA promotes best child welfare practices and supports the enhancement of children's rights throughout the world. Consistent with this effort, we find these standards to be compatible with and supportive of the United Nations Convention on the Rights of the Child, a blueprint for ensuring children's well-being and protections as a matter of right everywhere.

Bringing CWLA Standards to the Field

The CWLA National Blueprint articulates the ultimate goal for all children, youth, and families, and acknowledges that it will take the combined knowledge, skills, and resources of all systems, services, communities, and individuals to ensure that *all children will grow up safely, in loving families and supportive communities, with everything they need to flourish—and with connections to their culture, ethnicity, race, and language.* We encourage agencies, practitioners, advocates, and concerned citizens to use the standards as a vehicle for pursuing these fundamental goals.

CWLA will be developing readiness assessment and implementation tools to help with the implementation of the CWLA National Blueprint. To ensure the clarity needed for child welfare's role in achieving the vision, CWLA will continue with and update its program-specific Standards of Excellence within the context of the National Blueprint. We will use our programs, practice guidelines, publications, research, conferences, professional development, and consultation to provide further guidance. CWLA advocacy efforts will include nudging other systems, parents, and communities toward helping achieve the vision. Our children, youth, and families deserve no less.

Joseph M. Costa   Christine James-Brown
CWLA Board Chair   CWLA President/CEO

INTRODUCTION

Raising the Bar

The CWLA National Blueprint for Excellence in Child Welfare (CWLA National Blueprint or National Blueprint) presents a vision for the future of child welfare that all children will grow up safely in loving families and supportive communities. Although the formal child welfare system has a specific role to play as it relates to children who have been or are at risk of abuse and neglect, responsibility for the well-being of children and youth extends well beyond traditional child welfare organizations and services. While achieving the well-being of children and youth begins with their families, everyone—families, communities, providers, and organizations—has a responsibility for ensuring the safety, permanency, and well-being of all children and youth. This is essential for achieving excellence in child welfare. The CWLA National Blueprint applies to all children and youth, whether or not they receive child welfare services, and whether or not they have been identified as at risk for child abuse or neglect. This document is designed as a foundation upon which families, communities, providers, and other organizations can create the greatest opportunities for all children and youth to succeed and flourish.

The CWLA National Blueprint is intended to be a catalyst for change: to broaden the thinking of communities, individuals, and groups, including public and private organizations within and outside of the child welfare system, and to help them understand how their roles and responsibilities fit in the overall strategy to improve outcomes for children and youth. The National Blueprint also serves as the basis for updating and creating CWLA program-specific Standards of Excellence, which play a unique and pivotal role in moving child welfare practice forward.

The document's emphasis on engaging children, youth, families, and communities; breaking down barriers; and increasing the inter-connectedness of all involved will compel new ways of communicating and working together. Although families hold primary responsibility for protecting and raising children, communities provide the context for daily life, the cultural lens for translating information and experience, and the network of supports and connections that help children and youth overcome difficulties and become contributing members of society.

The CWLA National Blueprint focuses on maximizing the strengths and resilience of children, youth, and their nuclear, biological, extended, foster, and adoptive families within the context of their communities. By having youth and families be true partners in policymaking, planning, and funding decisions, communities and organizations can ensure that all children and youth are provided with the best opportunities for safe, healthy, nurturing environments for learning, growing, and becoming productive, healthy, fulfilled adults.

To help all children and youth flourish, society must provide services, supports, and resources so that families can ensure the safety, permanency, and well-being of their children with equal emphasis on all three. One cannot take precedence over another. Communities must be able to invest in the supports and services required to ensure that all children, youth, and families will have optimal opportunities to succeed. To facilitate community leadership and decisionmaking, current child welfare, education, social services, and health care systems will be required to transform their thinking and retool their mechanisms for allocating funds. Reform is required at the federal, tribal, state, and local levels, as is greater participation and investment from the foundation and corporate sectors.

Some of the CWLA National Blueprint's concepts are not new. While many entities will see their work reflected and validated herein, this document and its applicability to all children and youth adds levels of complexity that will present challenges and dilemmas in planning and actual implementation. Nonetheless, CWLA encourages everyone to aspire to achieving the standards detailed in the National Blueprint while recognizing that, for many organizations and communities, implementation will be neither straightforward nor swift. CWLA plans to develop and disseminate tools that will help identify strategies for implementation.

Organization and Format

The National Blueprint's organization is a departure from existing CWLA Standards of Excellence, which are clustered around traditional service areas. The CWLA National Blueprint includes a vision and values (page 21), and eight core principles (pages 22-23) and standards, which are built upon the vision, values, and principles.

Each of the eight principles heads a chapter containing standards relevant to that principle. Each standard is in bold font. Standards are followed by indented paragraphs that explain and clarify the standard.

To emphasize the interdependence among principles and standards, cross-references are included throughout the document. For example, the standards in the *Workforce* chapter must be understood in concert with the standards in the *Shared Responsibility and Leadership* chapter, and the standards in the *Supports and Services* chapter must be understood in the context of the *Rights of Children* chapter.

Important Points

Understanding all of the following key points aids readers in using the CWLA National Blueprint:

- All principles are equally important. They are not presented in order of priority.

- CWLA recommends that readers review the entire National Blueprint before concentrating on individual principles or standards. Many standards can be understood best when read in the context of other principles and standards. Cross-references are included throughout the document.

- Responsibility for implementation of the CWLA National Blueprint does not rest solely with traditional child welfare organizations, or with individual workers and supervisors within those organizations. Instead, responsibility for helping all children to flourish rests with their parents and families, with their communities, and with all adults in their lives.

- Definitions are included at the beginning of the CWLA National Blueprint to provide clarity about language in the context of this document. Every effort has been made to use terms consistently, and to avoid jargon.

- "Children" and "youth" are both defined, and are not synonymous and interchangeable. Most of the document refers to "children and youth." "Child" is used alone when applicable to people under age 18. "Youth" is used alone when a statement is not applicable to younger children.

- CWLA has developed accompanying documents such as an *Executive Summary* and *Frequently Asked Questions,* and will develop tools to facilitate implementation of the CWLA National Blueprint.

- Updates to current CWLA Standards of Excellence and development of future Standards of Excellence and Practice Guidelines relevant to child welfare will be based upon the CWLA National Blueprint.

How the CWLA National Blueprint Can Be Used

The CWLA National Blueprint may be used by:

- Policymakers, and community and organizational leaders, in:
  - Planning, organizing, and administering services;
  - Developing and revising policies and shaping policy discussions and initiatives;
  - Recruiting and orienting staff and board members;
  - Interpreting services to stakeholders, legislators, and organizations; and
  - Deciding upon and advocating for appropriate staffing and funding levels.
- Youth, parents, foster and adoptive parents, grandparents, and extended family members wanting more involvement in children's lives, advocating, seeking support or services, or offering support to others;
- Teachers, health and behavioral health care providers, childcare providers, coaches, social service and child welfare providers, youth group leaders, clergy, advocates, and others to validate and expand their efforts to help children and youth succeed and flourish;
- Advocates in their efforts to uphold children's rights, strengthen communities, and improve funding for supports and services;
- Elected and nonelected community leaders as they engage community members, collaborate with organizations and other communities, assess needs, and plan and develop supports and services;
- Federal, state, county, tribal, and local public officials, legislators, budget officers, foundation and corporate executives, and other entities allocating funds for services;

- Providers and communities as they establish desired outcomes, evaluate the performance of services and supports, and implement quality improvement models;

- Attorneys, court monitors, judges, and administrators in discovery and litigation;

- Educators and trainers revising curricula, academic programs, and organization-based training;

- Organizations making recommendations for systemic improvement, program development, and allocation of funds;

- Licensing specialists and regulatory bodies in establishing state, local, and tribal licensing requirements;

- Accrediting bodies, such as the Council on Accreditation (COA), the Joint Commission, the Commission on Accreditation of Rehabilitation Facilities (CARF), and the National Association for the Education of Young Children (NAEYC), as a foundation and reference for their accreditation standards;

- Researchers, evaluators, academics, and government entities for reference in journal articles, government reports, and research studies; and

- Federal entities, such as the Department of Health and Human Services, State Department, Department of Education, and General Accounting Office, as a basis for evaluating services, determining desired outcomes, and developing federal regulations that direct practice nationally and internationally.

Development Process

The National Blueprint was developed and vetted through the following inclusive process:

- CWLA convened an advisory committee of more than thirty (30) professionals representing child welfare agencies and organizations at federal, state, county, and community levels and with experience as policymakers, researchers, academicians, clinicians, workers, supervisors, parents (birth, foster and adoptive), advocates, foster care alumni, and members of the legal system. The Committee met twice for two-day, face-to-face meetings, during which members developed the parameters for the Vision, Principles, and Standards. Subgroups continued the Committee's work through a series of teleconferences.

- To align the National Blueprint with current evidence and best practices, CWLA staff completed a comprehensive review of relevant current research and provided a summary to the Committee to inform its work.

- Preliminary and second drafts were completed and reviewed by the Advisory Committee.

- CWLA invited individuals and organizations representing diverse stakeholders at federal, state, county, and local levels, in the public and private sectors, as well as tribal representatives, accrediting and regulatory bodies to review the third draft and provide critique through surveys, web-based conferences, and/or teleconferences.

- The CWLA Board of Directors approved the National Blueprint on March 8, 2013.

ACKNOWLEDGEMENTS

Writing Team:

Andrea Bartolo, Director of Consultation, CWLA

Julie Collins, MSW, LCSW, Director of Standards for Practice Excellence, CWLA

Etta Lappen Davis, MA, MEd, Consultant, Etsky Consulting

Linda Spears, Vice President, Policy and Public Affairs, CWLA

Advisory Committee:

Juanita Blount-Clark, Consultant, Center for the Study of Social Policy

Katharine H. Briar-Lawson, MSW, PhD, Dean and Professor, School of Social Welfare, University at Albany, State University of New York

Nadia Cayce, PhD Candidate, Parent Partner and Regional Technical Assistance Coordinator, Region I, TA Partnership

Crystal Collins-Camargo, MSW, PhD, Kent School of Social Work, University of Louisville

Eliza Cooper, Parent Partner

Terry Cross, Executive Director, National Indian Child Welfare Association

Lonna Davis, Director of Children's Programs, Futures Without Violence

Nicole Dobbins, Executive Director, Voice for Adoption

Darrell Evora, President and CEO, EMQ Families First

Mary Deffley Kurfess, LCSW-C, LICSW, MSSW, Associate, Office of Social Work Accreditation (OSWA), Council on Social Work Education

Jeremy C. Kohomban, PhD, President Harlem Dowling and President and CEO, The Children's Village

Ernesto Loperena, Executive Director, New York Council on Adoptable Children

Judge Maxwell Griffin, National Council of Juvenile & Family Court Judges

Heidi D. McIntosh, Senior Policy Advisor, Administration for Children, Youth, and Families/ACF/HHS

Linda Mitchell, Child Welfare Specialist, Children's Bureau/ACF/HHS

Jane Morgan, Director, Capacity Building Division, Children's Bureau/ACF/HHS

Jan Nisenbaum, Deputy Commissioner for Clinical and Program Services, Massachusetts Department of Children & Families

Nathan Nishimoto, Deputy Director, Orangewood Children & Family Services Agency

Adam Robe, CEO, Foster Care Alumni of America

Julie Rosicky, Executive Director, International Social Service, United States of America Branch, Inc.

Erika Tullberg MPA, MPH, Assistant Professor, New York University Child Study Center

Jorge Velazquez, Jr., MPA, Cultural Responsiveness Consultant, (formerly with the Child Welfare Academy, University of Maryland, School of Social Work)

Lisa von Pier, Assistant Commissioner, Division of Family and Community Partnerships and Division on Women, New Jersey Department of Children and Families

Robert Wentworth, Assistant Commissioner, Massachusetts Department of Children & Families

Jeff Whelan, Commissioner, Social Service Division, Saint Regis Mohawk Tribe

Charles Wilson, MSSW, Senior Director, Center for Developmental and Behavioral Services and Chadwick Center for Children and Families, Rady Children's Hospital

Joan Zlotnik, PhD, ACSW, Director of Social Work Policy Institute, National Association of Social Workers

CWLA Board Representatives:

Julie Sweeney Springwater, MSW, Vice-Chair

Lucille Echohawk, Member

Draft Reviewers:

Olivia Golden, Institute Fellow, Urban Institute

Kevin M. McGuire, Commissioner, Department of Social Services, Westchester County, New York

Ruth McRoy, PhD, Research Professor, Ruby Lee Piester Centennial Professor, The University of Texas, School of Social Work

Peter Pecora, PhD, Senior Director of Research Sciences, Casey Family Programs

CWLA Staff:

Rachel Adams, Editor

Lynda Arnold, Senior Fellow/Consultant

Christine James-Brown, President and CEO

Suzanne Lay, Government Affairs Associate

Donna D. Petras, PhD, MSW, Director, Models of Practice and Training

Marlene Saulsbury, Art Director

Special Acknowledgements

Special thanks goes to Etta Lappen Davis for her significant role in the writing of this document. She helped bring the ideas and suggestions to life. Her commitment, tenacity, and expertise helped to ensure that we met our deadlines and accomplished our goals.

We would also like to express our appreciation to all of the individuals and organizations that took the time to review the standards and provide us with feedback, including members of the CWLA National Commission on Practice Excellence, the CWLA National Commission on Public Policy, CWLA members, and other expert advisors.

DEFINITIONS

Abuse: The non-accidental commission of any act against an individual that causes or creates a substantial risk of harm or injury, or an act that constitutes a sexual offense under the laws of the jurisdiction in which it occurs.

Accountability: The extent to which an entity is answerable for its processes and outcomes to a variety of relevant internal and external stakeholders.

Advocacy: An act performed with or on behalf of others through direct intervention, empowerment, or representation. Case advocacy refers to actions taken in relation to a particular individual. Cause, social, or systems advocacy refers to actions taken in relation to a common issue affecting a group.

Behavioral Health Care: The application of medical, psychiatric, psychological, social work, and education principles and practices in the diagnosis and treatment of mental health and substance abuse disorders.

Benchmark: The quantifiable measurement of best practices in a sector or field to which entities can compare their own work and performance. For example, a benchmark for a community support organization might be the availability of brochures in each language spoken in the community.

Best Interests: Determinations made for the child's ultimate safety and well-being as the paramount concern, with consideration of a number of factors related to the circumstances of the child, including, but not limited to, the circumstances and capacity of the child's potential caregiver(s), the context of the prevailing community standard, and the child's opinions and preferences. Best interests considerations may be immediate, foreseeable, and/or lifelong.

Best Practices: Recommended services, supports, interventions, policies, or procedures based on current validated evidence, expert agreement, the opinions and values of the child, youth, or family, and the desired outcomes.

Child: A person under the age of 18.

Child Abuse: A non-accidental action that causes injury or harm to a child, regardless of whether it is considered "reportable" in the jurisdiction in which the event occurs.

Child Neglect: Child neglect occurs when a child is placed at risk of inadequate care by failure of an adult, who is responsible for the child's health or welfare, to intervene to eliminate that risk when the adult is able to do so and has or should have knowledge of the risk, regardless of whether it is reportable in the jurisdiction in which it occurs. This includes failure to provide needed food, clothing, shelter, medical care, supervision, or education that threatens the safety, health, or well-being of a child.

Child Welfare Agency: A government or tribal entity charged with protecting children from abuse and neglect.

Child Welfare System: A public child welfare entity and its workforce and network of providers and workforces responsible for protecting children, including: the entity that receives and investigates reports of suspected child maltreatment; providers of services to children and families to ameliorate past maltreatment and prevent future maltreatment; the organizations and providers that work to prevent child abuse and neglect; individuals who are mandated reporters; and the communities and community members that care for and about children, their safety, and their well-being. While the primary responsibility for child welfare rests with the states, the federal government plays a major role in supporting state child welfare systems in the delivery of supports and services.

Community: A social group of people that have certain commonalities. A community may be a group whose members reside in a specific locality, and share government, for example; a neighborhood, town, or city. A community may be a social, religious, occupational, or other group sharing common characteristics, heritage, or interests that perceives itself as distinct in some respect from the larger society within which it exists. For example: *the business community, the community of retirees, the foster parent community, or the LGBTQ community.*

Disparity: Unequal or unjust access to supports and services, or discrepancies in decisionmaking that may impact the experiences of individuals from racial and ethnic groups.

Disproportionality: Differences between the percentage of children, youth, and families of a certain racial or ethnic group in a geographic area and the percentage of that same group represented in systems such as child welfare, juvenile justice, special education, or mental health. Children, youth, and families from certain racial and ethnic groups may be overrepresented or underrepresented.

Emerging Practices: Specific approaches to problems or ways of working with particular people that are considered positive and effective by service recipients and/or providers, but that are too new or used too infrequently to have received general attention and have garnered scientific evidence.

Emotional Abuse: A pattern of behavior that impairs a child's emotional development or sense of self-worth. This may include constant criticism, threats, or rejection, as well as withholding love, support, or guidance. Emotional abuse is almost always present when other forms of abuse/neglect are identified.

Entity: Any person, unit, or group that has an independent, separate, or self-contained existence or identity. An entity can be an agency, government, organization, distinct community, or any other defined group.

Evidence-Based: Programs or practices that use the best available research and program and clinical expertise within the context of the child, family, and community characteristics, culture, and preferences. They are validated by scientific evidence that includes findings established through research, controlled studies, replication, or other valid methods of establishing evidence.

Evidence-Informed: Programs and practices that effectively integrate the best research evidence with clinical expertise, cultural competence, and the values of the persons receiving the services.

Experience as a Service Recipient: An individual's personal experiences that lead to an understanding fundamentally different from perceptions and understandings of people who have not had the same or similar experience.

Family-Focused: A perspective that focuses on the needs and welfare of individual family members within the context of their families. Family is defined broadly to include birth, blended, kinship, and foster and adoptive families.

Institutional Racism/Institutional Bias (also known as Systemic Racism or Bias): The presence of a societal norm in which policies, resources, and practices are designed to benefit some groups significantly more than others while simultaneously denying the existence of racism or bias as a variable. The institution or system fails to provide equal service or access and/or imposes additional requirements or penalties, based solely on color, culture, ethnicity, citizenship, country of origin, gender, religious background, or socioeconomic background.

Institutional racism and bias can be seen or detected in processes, attitudes, and behaviors that disadvantage any group through intentional or unintentional prejudice, ignorance, thoughtlessness, and stereotyping.

LGBTQ (Lesbian, Gay, Bisexual, Transgender, Questioning, or Queer): Includes those who identify as intersex, 2-spirit, or pansexual as well as those who identify as lesbian, gay, bisexual, transgender, questioning, or queer.

Maltreatment: An act or failure to act by an adult that results in physical abuse, neglect, medical neglect, sexual abuse, emotional abuse, or an act or failure to act which presents an imminent risk of harm to a child, regardless of whether the jurisdiction in which it occurs mandates reporting.

Mandated Reporter: An individual or entity required by law to report suspected abuse or neglect, as defined by the jurisdiction, to the appropriate authorities.

Organization: An entity with a recognized legal or business status. Organizations may be public or private, for-profit or nonprofit entities. Organizations may be advocacy groups, public agencies, providers that offer direct supports and services, funders, or business entities that support child well-being causes.

Physical Abuse: Type of maltreatment that refers to physical acts that caused or could have caused physical injury to the child.

Practice-Based Evidence: Real-life practices that provide the basis for inductively developing evidence—including anecdotal evidence, culturally-based interventions, and those grounded in tradition—that has not been validated by research. Practice-based evidence also includes adaptations of evidence-based practices that have been modified for a culture, age group, or other application for which they have not been researched.

Prevention: Efforts aimed at averting child abuse and neglect, or reducing unhealthy conditions and activities such as obesity, smoking, or substance abuse.

Promising Practices: Practices that have expert consensus or other support but that have not been as rigorously evaluated as those that are considered evidence-based or evidence-informed.

Protective Factors: Strengths and resources that appear to mediate or serve as a buffer against adverse experiences and risk factors that can decrease well-being. Protective factors include but are not limited to nurturing, attachment, positive relationships, family resilience, social connections, and concrete supports for caregivers.

Provider: Any individual or entity that provides direct supports or services to children, youth, and/or families.

Psychological Safety: The individual's perception concerning the consequences of taking interpersonal risks. It consists of beliefs about how others will respond when one reveals personal information, seeks information, reports a mistake, or proposes an idea or plan. Interpersonal trust is a prerequisite to psychological safety.

Public Entity: A government or tribal organization or body.

Resilience: The ability to adapt well to adverse experiences and to recover from trauma, tragedy, threats, or significant sources of stress. Resilience in children and youth enables them to thrive, mature, and increase competence in the midst of adverse circumstances.

Report: An allegation of maltreatment, abuse, or neglect made verbally and/or in writing to the appropriate investigative authority (typically this is the child protective services agency but in some jurisdictions it may also include law enforcement); or, a document that summarizes data and information.

Sexual Abuse: A type of maltreatment that refers to the involvement of the victim in sexual activity to provide sexual gratification or financial benefit to the perpetrator, including contacts for sexual purposes, molestation, statutory rape, prostitution, pornography, exposure, incest, or other sexually exploitative activities.

Stakeholder: An individual or group that has an interest in an entity's mission, performance, and outcomes. Stakeholders may include, but are not limited to: current and former service recipients, employees, volunteers, community representatives, governing bodies, advisory groups, funders, and regulators.

Strengths-Based: A perspective that emphasizes an individual or family's capabilities, success, support system, motivation to meet challenges, and previous experience in overcoming adversity.

System: A public entity and a defined network of providers that together address a specific need or service population. In most jurisdictions, there are multiple systems; for example, child welfare, juvenile justice, behavioral health, intellectual disabilities, education, public health, and employment. In other jurisdictions, there is a single social service or human service system that addresses multiple responsibilities. (See also *Child Welfare System* on page 14.)

Trauma: An experience or set of experiences that is emotionally painful, distressful, or shocking, which often results in lasting mental and physical effects; a serious or critical bodily injury, wound, or shock. A traumatic event is something life-threatening, very frightening, or life-altering that happens to or is witnessed by the individual. Examples include but are not limited to: fire, natural disaster, interpersonal violence, war, loss of a loved one, serious accident, and abuse.

Trauma-Informed: Having an understanding of how traumatic experience and traumatic stress affect human life, and an understanding of the vulnerabilities or triggers of trauma survivors that may be exacerbated.

Vendors: Individuals and organizations that are contracted by a system, public entity, community, or other funding source to provide supports and services.

Verbal Abuse: Verbal abuse is the use of words to cause harm. Verbal abuse may consist of shouting, insulting, intimidating, threatening, shaming, humiliating, demeaning, or other derogatory language.

Volunteers: Unpaid members of the workforce, including students and interns.

Well-Being: A state achieved as a result of having physical, educational, emotional, and psychological needs met. Indicators of well-being include reporting by an individual of his/her status and observations and opinions of others. Well-being is often viewed in terms of the absence of negative indicators.

Workforce: All persons in paid positions of any kind—whether they receive salaries, wages, or stipends—who are engaged in any aspect of service or support to children, youth, or families. The workforce also includes unpaid volunteers and interns working in organizations.

This broad definition includes people who may not think of themselves as child welfare workers.

Youth: An adolescent or young person through age 25. Youth under 18 are also children; youth over 18 are also adults.

VISION, VALUES, AND PRINCIPLES

VISION

All children will grow up safely, in loving families and supportive communities, with everything they need to flourish—and with connections to their culture, ethnicity, race, and language.

VALUES

We value children, youth, families, and communities. We believe in integrity, fairness, social justice, dignity, and honesty. We value these actions, qualities, and characteristics: respect, innovation, service, inclusiveness, collaboration, trust, flexibility, competence, and humility.

The vision, values, and principles are the foundation for the CWLA National Blueprint for Excellence in Child Welfare and are reflected throughout the document. The core principles are derived from the vision and values.

CORE PRINCIPLES

The following core principles guide the thinking, decisionmaking, and behavior of individuals, organizations, communities, and government entities committed to the promotion and enhancement of children's safety, permanency, and well-being.

Rights of Children

It is the responsibility of all members of society to work toward the shared goal of advancing the fundamental rights and needs of children.

Shared Responsibility and Leadership

Families, individuals, organizations, and communities share responsibility for assuring the safety and well-being of children and youth. To help children and youth flourish, leaders at every level and in all realms ensure that individuals, families, communities, organizations, and systems collaborate, communicate, create and nurture meaningful partnerships.

Engagement/Participation

Children, youth, and families are engaged and empowered to promote family success and build community capacity. Service providers and organizations acknowledge, appreciate, and validate the voices and experiences of those whose lives they touch so that responsive community-based resources and services are developed, nurtured, and sustained.

Supports and Services

Families, individuals, communities, organizations, and systems protect children from abuse and neglect, and provide an array of supports and services that help children, youth, and their families to accomplish developmental tasks, develop protective factors, and strengthen coping strategies.

Quality Improvement

Services and supports are designed and implemented based on evidence and knowledge, data collection is meaningful and focused on measuring outcomes and achieving success, continuous quality improvement is emphasized and supported, and innovative practices and programs are encouraged.

Workforce

The workforce consists of competent, skilled people with a variety of experiences and representing various disciplines. They are committed to high-quality service delivery and are provided with the training, tools, resources, and support necessary to perform their roles effectively.

Race, Ethnicity, and Culture

Individuals, families, communities, organizations, and systems work together to understand and promote equality, cultural humility, and strong racial, cultural, and ethnic identity, while showing consideration for individual differences and respecting the sovereign rights of tribes.

Funding and Resources

Funding decisions in the private sector and at federal, state, local, and tribal levels are informed by the certainty that the well-being of children, families, and communities are interconnected, and that sufficient and equitable funding is essential to the well-being of all of them.

CWLA
NATIONAL BLUEPRINT
FOR EXCELLENCE IN CHILD WELFARE

I. Rights of Children

PRINCIPLE

It is the responsibility of all members of society to work toward the shared goal of advancing the fundamental rights and needs of children.

Too many children in this country face obstacles to realizing their full potential and need access to services, supports, and protections. Therefore, all members of society have a responsibility to advocate for and work toward the affirmation and protection of children's rights and to ensure that their best interests are considered in all decisions affecting them.

To meet the needs of all children, and especially those who are vulnerable, CWLA recommends children's rights and policies that are broader than existing legal requirements. As will all standards, advocates are encouraged to work toward the implementation of these rights and policies. Each individual and entity will need to determine the interface with and applicability of relevant laws, and the extent to which it can and should move beyond current law regarding the rights of children.

The rights of children cannot be advanced in isolation. Rather, children's rights must reflect and respect the critical roles and responsibilities of the parents and family members who care for them. In most instances, parents are uniquely qualified to advance the rights of children and to act in their best interest. As such, parents are afforded the right to raise their child according to their beliefs; however, they may not violate the fundamental rights of that child. As such, the rights of children and parents are interconnected. It is the responsibility of every parent, family, and caregiver to recognize and protect children's rights, and it is the responsibility of individuals and entities to work together to give families/parents optimum tools, supports, and opportunities so that they can fully assume responsibility for advancing the rights of their children.

Children's rights belong equally to each and every child, regardless of race, color, age, disability, gender, familial status, religion, sexual orientation, gender identity, genetic information, language, religion, nationality, ethnic or social origin, political beliefs, citizenship, or any other status or condition in life.

The rights of children are applied differently depending on their ages and developmental abilities. Likewise, the ability of children to understand and respect the rights of parents is commensurate with their age and abilities. Adults should tailor the issues they discuss and the way in which they answer questions to the age and maturity of the individual child.

STANDARDS

SURVIVAL AND DEVELOPMENT

I.1. Children should have access to food, clean and safe water, shelter, and clothing required for survival and healthy development.

Adults must meet children's basic needs because children do not typically have the resources or ability to provide for their own basic needs.

Poor nutrition puts children at risk for lifelong health issues; creating lasting disadvantages and challenges. Hunger is an obstacle to learning. Without proper nutrition, children are distracted and physically unable to succeed in the classrooms.

Water is essential to life, and all children must have access to clean, fresh water for drinking and bathing. (See also *Safe and Healthy Communities* on page 61.)

Each child must have a place to live and sufficient clothing for warmth, cleanliness, and safety. Homelessness is a source of toxic stress.

I.2. Children should have nurturing and loving families.

All children should have home lives that provide support for the whole child. Loving, nurturing, and caring environments provide children the necessary foundation to feel self-assured and self-actualized.

Children have a right for their families to receive the support and services needed to preserve the family.

I.3. Children should have connections with their family and communities.

Children have the right to live with their families of origin unless living with their families is harmful to them. When a child cannot live with both parents, the child has a right to be connected with both parents unless connection with one of the parents would be harmful to the child. The child also has a right to know parents, siblings, and extended family, and to maintain connections with their extended family. A child whose parents reside in different countries should have the right to maintain relationships and contact with both parents and other family members. Governments should respect the right of the child and his/her parents to leave the country and reenter the country, unless restrictions are necessary to protect the child or the public's health and safety.

It should be understood that the child's right to be connected with family is not precluded by decisions that a child be raised by a single parent, a same-sex couple, grandparents, adoptive parent(s), or any other family configuration. Regardless of any decisions about the child's living arrangement and family constellation, the child has a right to be connected with his/her original parents. When connection is not possible, or is not in the child's best interests, the child has a right to know about his/her original parents.

When a child is adopted, the child has rights to connections with and awareness of both the original family and the adoptive family.

When siblings cannot live with their family, they should be placed together unless there is a clear rationale for why it is not in their best interests. Separated siblings have a right to visit each other and to maintain contact.

Children have a right to maintain connections with their communities—schools, friends, neighbors, special people, and places they are connected to—even when they are required to move from where they are living.

I.4. Children should have access to information about their family history and background information.

Access to and understanding of family history is vital for children's development and sense of self. Such access is also important for understanding family medical history.

I.5. Children should be able to preserve their racial, ethnic, cultural, and religious identity.

Children have a right to understand their heritage; to preserve their connections to culture and religion; to learn and preserve their traditions; and to have adults and peers support their development of strong and healthy racial, ethnic, cultural, and religious identity.

I.6. Children should be able to have their own gender identity and sexual orientation.

Children begin to develop gender identify in the first year of life; by age three, most children clearly understand whether they are male or female, and by age four, gender identity is firmly established. [i]

I.7. Children should have access to formal education.

Children have a right to education with the resources, skills, and contributions necessary for the survival and full development of the child. Each child has the right to develop to his or her full potential.

Early childhood education is particularly important for ensuring school readiness. Children should be given access to early childhood and school programs that respond to their social, emotional, psychological, physical, academic, and creative needs.

Children living in poverty should have the same opportunities for quality educational as children living in communities of high economic status. Studies of education outcomes in the United States consistently document a correlation between poverty and poor education. [ii]

Children should be encouraged to complete high school and continue with post-secondary education. Children with poor achievement and those identified as at risk for dropping out of school should be provided with additional supports to complete school.

I.8. Children should have access to quality health care.

Each child should be provided with health care based on practical, scientifically sound, methods, and technology. [iii] Health care should include promotion of health, early diagnosis of disease or disability, prevention of disease, immunizations, access to medicines, when needed, regular check-ups, dental care, and behavioral health care. Health care should be accessible, age-appropriate, and responsive to the child's culture. No child should be denied access to these resources for a healthy childhood.

I.9. Children should be able to live in a safe physical environment that is free from pollutants and toxins.

Children should live in homes, neighborhoods, and communities that are free from hazards. Communities should be free from environmental degradation. Communities have the responsibility to identify risks, develop plans to ameliorate them, and seek governmental and other assistance to correct them.

I.10. Children should have access to leisure, cultural, and recreational activities; and to healthy social relationships.

Children should be able to engage in play and recreational

activities appropriate to their age and development. Children should have opportunities to engage in cultural and artistic experiences and activities.

Each community should have safe play and recreational spaces that encourage children to engage in indoor and outdoor physical activities, as well as other activities that are social and fun.

Each community should encourage the provision of appropriate and equal opportunities for cultural, artistic, recreational, and leisure activity, as well as opportunities for children to develop friendships with peers and positive social contacts with adults.

PROTECTION

I. 11. Children must be protected from abuse, neglect, maltreatment, exploitation, and abduction.

These rights include protection from all forms of child abuse, neglect, exploitation, and cruelty, including the right to special protection in times of war.

Children have a right to protection from abuse within the criminal justice system. Children and youth in the juvenile justice system should have the same rights as all children.

Children should not be charged or incarcerated as adults.

Children should be protected from kidnapping and trafficking. Children should not be moved across state lines or out of the country illegally.

Children who are undocumented immigrants have the same human rights as all children. Rights are independent of citizenship or immigration status.

It is the responsibility of governments to legislate these protections and enforce societal adherence to its responsibility to protect children. It is also the responsibility of governments to intervene on behalf of children when parents or other caregivers violate their rights to protection. Each jurisdiction should have forms of prevention, and systems for identification, reporting, referral, investigation, treatment, and follow-up of instances of child maltreatment described above, and, as appropriate, for judicial involvement.

I.12. Children should be protected from discrimination on the basis of race, color, age, disability, gender, familial status, religion, sexual orientation, gender identity, genetic information, language, religion, national, ethnic or social origin, political beliefs, or citizenship.

Children should not be treated unfairly on any basis, whatever their race, religion, or abilities; whatever they think or say; and whatever their family background or family constellation. It does not matter where children live, what language they speak, what their parents do, what gender they are, what their culture is, whether they have a disability, or whether they are rich or poor. All children should be protected from discrimination.

I.13. Children must be protected under the law.

Children have the right to representation in the courts of law, and to advocates when their welfare is a matter of concern for the court. Advocates should be well-informed and objective adults charged with protecting each child's well-being and rights throughout the court process.

I.14. Children must be protected from torture or other cruel, inhumane, or degrading treatment or punishment.

Every organization and provider serving children and youth should have pro-social behaviorial support and intervention policies and procedures that prohibit cruel, inhumane, and degrading treatment or punishment. Children should not be humiliated.

When children commit offenses, neither capital punishment nor life imprisonment without the possibility of release should be imposed. Charging and incarcerating children as adults is cruel and inhuman treatment.

Each community should have an anti-bullying program that educates children, youth, and adults about the effects of bullying and steps to eliminate bullying. (See also *Supports and Services* on page 59.)

I. 15. Children should be protected from corporal punishment.

Children have a right to be protected from corporal punishment in every setting in which they live, learn, and receive supports and services.

Research regarding the harmful effects of physical discipline/corporal punishment on the well-being of children and youth is extensively documented.[iv][v][vi] Parents, caregivers, and other adults do not have the right to harm children.

It is a basic premise of human rights that one individual's rights may not be used to harm another or to violate another's rights.

I. 16. Children must have decisions made in their best interests.

The best interests of children are paramount; they must be the primary concern in making decisions that may affect children. All adults and all organizations should work toward doing what is best for the child. When a child's parents cannot make decisions that are in the best interests of the child, other adults are responsible for assisting. Adults, particularly lawmakers and those who set budget and policy, should consider how their decisions will affect children.

All adults making decisions concerning children should understand that there is not a template for determining children's best interests. What is in the best interest of one child might not be the same for another child. Each situation should be examined carefully, and all relevant factors should be considered before a determination of best interests is made. (See also *Engagement/Participation* on page 49.)

I.17. Children should be protected from interference with their privacy.

All parents, caregivers, and guardians are responsible for protecting children's privacy.

No child should be subjected to arbitrary or unlawful interference with his or her privacy, family, or correspondence, or to unlawful attacks on his or her honor and reputation.

All children's service providers should ensure the privacy and protection of the children they serve. They should have clear written policies and procedures for balancing a child's right to privacy with the responsibility to protect the child and to act in the child's best interests. Policies and procedures for privacy protection should be in compliance with applicable laws concerning records, Internet privacy, and parent and guardian access to information concerning their children. (See also *Social Media and Technology* on page 74).

PARTICIPATION

I.18. Children should be involved in all aspects of decisionmaking regarding plans for them.

Children are entitled to express their opinions and to have a say in matters affecting their lives. They have the right to be heard and to have their opinions considered fully. They should be included in decisions about their future.

Depending upon the age and development of a child, it may be necessary for adults to present the child's point of view, help the child prepare for a meeting or court hearing, intervene on the child's behalf, or modify decisions.

Children should have the opportunity to ask questions, share their thoughts and feelings, and be present at meetings/hearings related to them. In rare instances when this is not possible, the child's wishes should be relayed, in person or in writing, by an advocate, case manager, therapist, or other adult.

Through engaging their rights to participate, children are helped to understand self-determination and be prepared for active roles in society.

I.19. Children should be able to express themselves freely.

Children have the right to freedom of expression. This right should include freedom to seek, receive, and impart information and ideas of all kinds—orally, in writing or in print, in the form of art, or through any other media of a child's choice.

The exercise of this right may be subject to certain restrictions, but these should only be such restrictions as are provided by law and are necessary to respect the rights or reputations of others, or to protect the health or safety of the child or others.

RESOURCES

Child Rights International Network, http://www.crin.org/

Privacy Rights Clearinghouse, Fact Sheet 21a: Children's Safety on the Internet, https://www.privacyrights.org/fs/fs21a-childrensafety.htm

UNICEF, http://www.unicef.org/index.php

Summary of UN Rights of the Child in Child Friendly Language, http://www.unicef.org/southafrica/SAF_resources_crcchildfriendly.pdf

CWLA

NATIONAL BLUEPRINT

FOR EXCELLENCE IN CHILD WELFARE

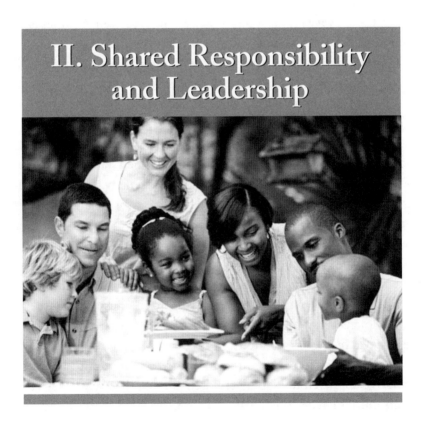

II. Shared Responsibility and Leadership

PRINCIPLE

Families, individuals, organizations, and communities share responsibility for assuring the safety and well-being of children and youth. To help children and youth flourish, leaders at every level and in all realms ensure that individuals, families, organizations, and systems collaborate, communicate, create, and nurture meaningful partnerships.

Responsibility must be shared among professionals and non-professionals, among community members and non-community members, across disciplines, and among all entities. It takes everyone, working together, to create environments and communities within which children and youth can flourish.

Where children live affects their development, well-being, and life chances. It is essential, therefore, to ensure that the strengths and resources of communities are fully utilized to achieve the safety and well-being of children and youth.

An imperative foundation of *Shared Responsibility* is that supports and services must occur WITH youth and their families. Supports and services can no longer be considered things that happen TO children, youth, and families. This concept is explored in the *Engagement/Participation* section of the CWLA National Blueprint. (See page 45.)

A multitude of well-integrated services and supports is essential to the emotional well-being and success of children, youth, and families. Access to needed supports and services is often crucial to the survival of individuals and families who are most vulnerable, and sometimes, to the survival of their communities.

Strong leadership is required to ensure a community-based collaborative approach to helping children and youth succeed. This leadership must include individuals with experience as service recipients (sometimes referred to as "lived" experience)—i.e. parents, children, youth, or extended family members, in addition to qualified professionals with credentials.

Leaders must be "honest, forward-looking, inspiring and competent."[vii] Leaders should demonstrate characteristics appropriate for the positions they hold, and should be accountable to their communities and entities. (See also *Workforce* on page 93 and *Quality Improvement* on page 80.)

STANDARDS

COMMUNITIES

II.1. **Community members (such as elders, leaders, and representatives) should have participatory roles at all levels and in all aspects of work with children, youth, and families.**

Community members should be an integral part of assessing community strengths and needs, designing programs, determining contract awards, identifying intended outcomes, reviewing and evaluating existing supports and services, and establishing partnerships.

II.2. **Community members should be present on governing boards, executive/management positions, advisory boards, task forces, committees, and focus groups, and should have an equal voice and decisionmaking power.**

Families and organizations exist within the context of a community; the community environment plays a crucial role for the family. Each community's culture impacts families in particular ways. For systems and communities to be truly responsive to the needs of children, youth, and families, community leaders and representatives from all sectors (e.g. faith-based, business, professional) should come together to create and guide appropriate and responsive community environments and service development and delivery. Community members should assist with the identification of strengths and needs of the community. They should help non-community members to understand the community's culture, identify and build on the community's strength, and participate in ways that are culturally appropriate for that community.

LEADERSHIP

II.3. **Leaders are responsible for building the capacity of their entities and communities to respond to the needs of children, youth, and families.** (See also *Workforce* on page 93 and *Engagement/Participation* on page 46.)

Leaders have a responsibility for and to children, youth, and families. Leaders must lead and represent simultaneously, a sometimes-precarious balancing act that requires foresight, critical thinking, expert negotiation, and powers of persuasion.

To help their entities and communities provide everything children and youth need to flourish, leaders must have the ability to assess needs, know how to work collaboratively within and across communities and systems, understand their own strengths and limitations and the strengths and limitations of their entities. Leaders must be able to help individuals and groups to build their capacity to move in desirable directions and to make positive change.

Leaders must have the ability to build and rebuild relationships between and among local residents, local associations, and local institutions and between communities and external entities and resources.[viii]

II.4. **Leaders are responsible for creating environments that build and support the hardiness and resilience among employees, volunteers, and communities.**

To survive and thrive while providing supports and services to children, youth, and families, workers and supervisors must be psychologically hardy[ix][x] and resilient. The growing body of research on workforce stress and exposure to trauma, including exposure to the trauma experiences of children, youth, and families, compels all leaders' to act. The research points to the important role leaders have in ensuring their workforce is resilient and hardy. By being hardy and resilient, staff are better able to cope with stress of the work. When they do experience stress symptoms from working with children, youth, and families that have experienced trauma (also known as secondary traumatic stress), leaders ensure the work environment supports them in addressing this and improving their ability to cope in the future. Quality leaders have a responsibility to recognize and acknowledge the "hazards of the work" and create environments that model and support their staff being hardy and resilient so that they are able to thrive and flourish. (See also *Secondary Traumatic Stress and Burnout* on page 103.)

COLLABORATION

II.5. **Each community, entity, individual, and system should recognize that collaborative and cooperative relationships are essential to creating and sustaining the supports and services needed by children, youth, and families.**

Collaborative and cooperative relationships are necessary within entities, between entities, and between entities and the community. Successful collaboration requires breaking down barriers, ensuring open and effective communication, addressing differences in philosophy, and developing common goals and direction.

True collaboration "is combining resources from two or more agencies to achieve results they cannot achieve by themselves." Collaborations can be both formal and informal.

II.6. There should be effective and meaningful partnership between the public and private sectors. To provide seamless integration of supports and services, systems should be designed to build on the individual and collective strengths of all partners.

Public entities, private entities, and communities should work together to modify current models of bidding and contracting, which often emphasize competition rather than collaboration. Competition without collaboration is not conducive to success in meeting the needs of children, youth, and families.[xiii] When entering into contracts to support the collaborative process, primary consideration should be given to the quality of supports and services.

Public entities and their private partners should work together to develop seamless systems. There should be mechanisms for simplifying points of entry and for sharing information and data across systems. Shared vision, shared outcomes, and outcome measures are essential to achieving partnerships.

All partners should participate in planning and evaluation of the best configuration of public-private distribution of responsibility, programs, and services. There should be full consideration of systemic, public entity, and private entity strengths; relevant performance history; financial resources; and involvement of the community. (See also *Communities* on page 39, and *Funding and Resources* on page 120.)

GOVERNANCE AND CAPACITY

II.7. Each entity, regardless of size, should have a governance structure that emphasizes sound policy and procedure, transparency and accountability, and information sharing.

Sound governance structure and practices are critical to the underpinning and strategic direction of all entities and their capacity to operate within a multicultural, sociopolitical, and economically turbulent environment.

While there are differences among entities depending upon variables such as mission, size, public, private, statutory, non-statutory, urban, rural, and community, the need for good governance is universal. There are many excellent resources available on effective governance models and strategies.

At a minimum, each entity should have: [xiv]

- A responsible governance body;

- A mission and philosophy that captures the entity's dedication to its services and those served;

- A plan for accomplishing its mission;

- Intended outcomes, and the processes for achieving them (See also *Quality Improvement* on page 80);

- Careful personnel recruitment and selection (See also *Workforce* on page 94);

- Reasonable workloads and adequate clerical support (See also *Workforce* on page 100);

- High-quality ongoing coaching, monitoring, and supervision (See also *Workforce* on page 101);

- Wise use of essential technology (See also *Social Media and Technology* on page 74); *SM Policy, Remote access Policy Elect wkst. Policy*

- Organizational standards of quality, expected results, and performance measurement (See also *Quality Improvement* on page 81);

- Risk management system, including adequate insurance; and

- Excellent communication among governance members, leadership, and workforce (See also *Shared Responsibility and Leadership* on page 40, *Workforce* on page 95 and *Positive Culture* and *Climate* on page 99).

RESOURCES

Supervisor Training Project at the National Child Welfare Resource Center for Organizational Improvement, http://muskie.usm.maine.edu/helpkids/supervision-projectabout.htm

Mitchell, L., Walters, R., Thomas, M.L. Denniston, J., McIntosh, H., & Brodowski, M. (2012). The Children's Bureau's Vision for the Future of Child Welfare. *Journal of Public Child Welfare*, 6(4), 550-567. Retrieved from http://dx.doi.org/10.1080/15548732.2012.715267.

NATIONAL BLUEPRINT

FOR EXCELLENCE IN CHILD WELFARE

III. Engagement/Participation

PRINCIPLE

Children, youth, and families are engaged and empowered to promote family success and build community capacity. Service providers and organizations acknowledge, appreciate, and validate the voices and experiences of those whose lives they touch, so that responsive community-based resources and services are developed, nurtured, and sustained.

There must be partnership with children, youth, and families in order to create communities, prevention mechanisms, and service delivery entities that nurture flourishing children, youth, and families for generations to come. It is essential to have positive strategies and approaches to effectively engage children, youth, families, and the communities in which they live. The public systems cannot stand apart from the communities in which they function. (See also *Shared Responsibility and Leadership* on page 41.)

STANDARDS

POSITIVE ENGAGEMENT STRATEGIES

III. 1. Every entity should use strength-based and family-focused approaches in their work.

How children, youth, and families are approached is critical to achieving positive outcomes. Positive approaches demonstrate a commitment to family well-being, facilitating an environment that is trusting and safe, and in which families and professionals can share successes and challenges. (See also *Meeting Basic Needs* on page 62 and *Psychological Safety* in the following standard.)

Positive outcomes are most likely when children, youth, and families are engaged with cultural sensitivity and responsiveness; with an understanding of their histories and paths to the present; and with a desire to ensure their psychological safety, recognize their rights and their need to make choices, and partner with them.

When relevant, each member of the family, all other members of the household, and, whenever possible, extended family members, should be asked about family strengths. They can often identify strengths that may not be readily apparent to outsiders.

III.2. **Every entity should work to ensure that families feel physically and psychologically safe. This can be done by asking families what is needed for their psychological safety.**

A person who has experienced/is experiencing traumatic stress may not be able to engage without first feeling safe. While physical safety is essential, it often is not enough to help an individual feel safe. It is also essential to ask a person what is needed for them to feel psychologically safe.

A family's story provides the context for how they currently function and the basis for understanding how best to respond/ provide support. Each family's story should be treated with dignity and respect.

Whether or not families identify what makes them feel safe, the following efforts within the family unit and by people outside the family may be helpful in establishing psychological safety:

- Listening to each family member;

- Demonstrating respect and empathy for family members;

- Developing an understanding of the family's past experiences, current situation, concerns, and strengths;

- Understanding what reminds them of trauma they have experienced;

- Creating opportunities for choice;

- Responding to concrete needs quickly;

- Establishing the purpose of involvement with the family;

- Getting input from the community in order to ensure efforts are responsive;

- Being aware of one's own biases and prejudices;

- Providing clear expectations of change; and

- Being consistent, reliable, and honest.

TRAUMA-INFORMED ENGAGEMENT

III.3. Entities should use trauma-informed approaches, asking what has happened to individuals and families instead of asking what is wrong with them.

When using a trauma lens, entities recognize that many children, youth, and families have experienced and/or are experiencing trauma. Using trauma-informed approaches can help to ensure their psychological and physical safety. From the initial contact with an individual or family, and throughout the process of working with them, staff and volunteers should encourage sharing, and respect their story and feelings. Indeed, research shows that relationships can contribute to their healing process and allow the stress reflexes of "fight, flight, or freeze"[xv] to subside.

Trauma-informed approaches help establish an environment of trust, gain an objective understanding of family dynamics, determine the right supports and services for individuals and families, and give participants the opportunity to write a new story.

Experiencing any type of trauma, especially repeated and ongoing traumatic stress, can have a serious impact on children's development and can have a lifelong impact. In addition to requiring an understanding of the psychological effects of trauma and traumatic stress, trauma-informed approaches require an understanding of the impact on the developing brain and children's neurodevelopment.

Trauma-informed approaches are especially beneficial for engaging families with mental health issues and histories of traumatic loss, substance abuse, and domestic violence.[xvii][xviii] (See also *Trauma-Informed Approaches* on page 69.)

YOUTH AND FAMILY INVOLVEMENT

III. 4. Each entity should fully engage youth and families in all aspects of the work, including program design and development, policy and procedure development, hiring, staff orientation and training, practice guidelines, evaluation, and quality improvement processes. (See also *Workforce* on page 96 and *Quality Improvement* on page 80.)

Each entity should have a parent and youth participation process that actively involves them as partners, cultivates and uses their leadership skills, and encourages their participation in case and/or issues advocacy. Youth and families should be asked how they want to be involved, and what, to them, constitutes meaningful involvement. These opportunities should be well communicated to stakeholders and to the general public. Communities and other entities should recognize that engagement of youth and families means bringing ideas and input to the table that leaders and staff may never have considered.

All individuals within the entity should be trained in youth and family engagement strategies. (See also the following standard.)

Each entity should have an active youth and family advocacy program that is well-communicated to all children, youth, and families involved with the entity, as well as to the community at large.

EXPERIENCE AS A SERVICE RECIPIENT

III.5. People with experience as service recipients or family members of service recipients should serve as mentors; help to educate those working with children, youth, and families; and serve on governing and/or advisory boards.

To best engage children, youth, and families, people with experience as a service recipient should be involved and visible at many levels of each entity. (See also *Shared Responsibility and Leadership* on page 38, *Workforce* on page 94, and the aforementioned standard.)

Communities and other entities should have mentoring programs that encourage families to seek and give advice to their peers. Family members who have already navigated the challenges of seeking support or receiving services may be able to provide guidance and direction, unavailable from other sources, to children, youth, their parents, and extended family members.

Mentoring or other peer programs may allow families to be more receptive to developing skills such as coping with stress or job training and hunting, and to receiving supports and services, than they might otherwise be. Receptivity is an essential factor in families' building the skills they need to nurture and care for their children. (See also *Supports and Services* on page 63.)

DEVELOPING TRUST, BUILDING RELATIONSHIPS

III.6. Everyone should recognize that having a trusting relationship is preliminary to engagement.

To engage children, youth, and families, staff and volunteers must build trust. Building trust and relationships provides hope and reduces barriers to effective engagement. Children, youth, and families should not be expected to divulge personal, private information to people they do not trust. Trust may be based on an individual's behavior and reputation, and/or the reputation and previous activity of a public entity, organization, or provider.

To build trust, organizations and individuals must be regarded as trustworthy and ethical. Toward that end, the following actions can aid in establishing individual and organizational trustworthiness:

- Communicate openly and clearly in a language the family understands;

- Respect boundaries;

- Be empathic;

- Communicate warmth;

- Recognize strengths;

- Be open-minded;

- Acknowledge feelings;

- Schedule meetings at times when children, youth, and families can be available;

- Make documents available in language that children, youth, and families understand;

- Provide translators if necessary to facilitate communication;

- Do not rush meetings and visits;

- Ask about family norms and cultural traditions; and

- Give families, children, and youth your undivided attention.

YOUTH ENGAGEMENT

III.7. Youth should be included in the process of designing and creating programs, developing, reviewing, and revising policies and procedures, as well as quality improvement processes and program evaluation. Youth should be involved in all aspects of their own planning and decisionmaking. (See also *Rights of Children* on page 34 and with the aforementioned standard.)

Youth are more likely to engage when they feel heard, and when their opinions are valued.

Each entity should commit itself to including, as appropriate, youth with experience as a service recipient on advisory boards, task forces, focus groups, Boards of Directors, and other decisionmaking capacities.

When participating in supports and services, youth often have remarkably different perspectives on what they need, want, and should set as priorities than do the adults around them.

Adults who have had experience as a service recipient during their youth can contribute the additional perspective they have gained, having entered adulthood and having moved beyond adolescent needs and wants.

PARENTAL AND EXTENDED FAMILY ENGAGEMENT

III.8. Parents and extended family members should be included in all aspects of planning and decisionmaking about them and their children.

Families should be encouraged and supported in engaging in all aspects of their children's lives, such as meetings, service planning, and court hearings, school or child care events, and day-to-day activities.

Entities should ask children, youth, and their parents or legal guardians which family members and other supports they wish to include. Those people should be engaged, whenever possible, unless contraindicated. (See also *Rights of Children* on page 34.)

When parents live in a different country, extra effort is needed and should be expended to maintain contact, arrange for visits, and involve them in the lives of their children. (See also *Rights of Children* on page 34.)

Extra effort may also be required when children and parents are within the same state or country but are separated by significant distance.

When in-person contact is not possible or not frequent enough, parents and other family members should have contact with children through social media and other electronic communication options, unless contraindicated.

Complete background information should be obtained from as many family members as possible, so that children and youth can have accurate, truthful family medical and social history. (See also *Rights of Children* on page 29.)

There are many reasons why family members may have lost touch and connection, including separation of siblings in care, migration and immigration, incarceration, divorce, and remarriage. It is important to identify reasons and help the family work thorough them.

When contact with immediate family members has been lost, family-finding strategies[xix] should be used to locate them, unless contraindicated because of safety. As needed, counseling should be provided to each family member to help reestablish contact. It is especially crucial to use family finding when identification and location of a family member could help a child avoid unnecessary foster care placement.

FATHERS

III.9. All efforts should be made to include fathers throughout their children's involvement with supports and services. (See also *Parental and Extended Family Engagement.*)

Research supports the importance of engagement of the fathers in the lives of their children.[xx]

Each entity should consider the needs of fathers and families being served, and should identify fathers' interests, and any barriers and impediments to their involvement with their children and engagement with staff.

Entities should make sure office and waiting area environments are welcoming to men. For instance, there should be magazines, literature, furnishings, and décor that are as welcoming to men as to women. Father-friendly services should be provided to fathers to help with parenting skills or to help them with basic needs to ensure that their children can safely remain in their homes.

Single fathers should be afforded the same family preservation services and supports as are afforded single mothers.

Special outreach and engagement efforts should be made when fathers are incarcerated. Incarcerated fathers of infants and young children should have opportunities to see their children often, and to actively parent.

MOTHERS

III.10. All efforts should be made to include mothers throughout their children's involvement with supports and services. (See also *Parental and Extended Family Engagement.*)

Mother-friendly strategies should be used to engage each mother in all aspects of her child's life, such as meetings, service planning, and court hearings, as well as, school and child care events and day-to-day activities.

Women should be encouraged to obtain prenatal care throughout pregnancy and should be provided with supports and services to engage them in giving their babies a healthy start in life.

Mothers should have access to information about breastfeeding and should be encouraged to nurse their babies. Young mother programs, healthy infant programs, and home-visiting programs are successful models for engaging young and first-time mothers and helping them to develop nurturing relationships with their children.

Incarcerated mothers of infants and young children should have opportunities to see their children often, continue nursing infants, and actively parent. Community-based, non-prison programs can offer mothers serving sentences the opportunity to parent while completing restitution. [xxi]

CULTURALLY APPROPRIATE ENGAGEMENT AND RESPONSE

III. 11. Each entity should use culturally appropriate strategies to engage and respond to children, youth, and families. (See also *Culturally Informed and Diverse* on page 112.)

It is essential for each entity use engagement strategies that are appropriate for the people involved in their supports or services. Consideration of cultural norms, sexual orientation, language barriers, culturally based biases, and dietary restrictions can be crucial for engagement. Ignoring culturally based norms can result in barriers and impediments to engagement.

Entities should make sure office and waiting area environments are welcoming to everyone. Multiculturalism and cultural competence should be evident in postings (in relevant languages) décor, and magazines.

A diverse, multilingual, multicultural staff helps families to engage.

COMMITMENT OF WORKFORCE AND LEADERSHIP

III.12. The leadership and workforce of each entity and community should be committed to active engagement of children, youth, and families in responding to needs within communities. (See also *Workforce* on page 95 and *Shared Responsibility and Leadership* on page 39.)

To assure that leaders at all levels have the necessary knowledge and competencies to engage children, youth, and families, each entity should establish and adhere to child, youth, and family engagement criteria for its leadership and workforce positions.

In order to be effective, the workforce should hear and learn from people they are serving. The workforce must be open to doing so, and must be willing and able to engage with children, youth, and families in a meaningful way.

do we add specific language to job specs?

RESOURCES

Assessing the Impact of InsideOut Dad™ on Newark Community Education Centers (CEC) Residential Reentry Center Residents, Executive Summary. Rutgers University-Newark Economic Development Research Group, School of Public Affairs and Administration (2011)

Child Welfare Information Gateway Fact Sheet on Family Engagement (2010), http://www.childwelfare.gov/pubs/f_fam_engagement

Harvard Research on Family Engagement, http://www.hfrp.org/family-involvment/informing-family-engagement-policy

National Resource Center for Permanency and Family Connection – Family Engagement Toolkit, http://www.hunter.cuny.edu/socwork/nrcfcpp/fewpt/

Connecting Families and Schools: An Assessment Tool for Educators Working with Culturally and Linguistically Diverse Students, http://web.multco.us/sites/default/files/sun/documents/connectingfamilyandschool.pdf

Engaging Families as Experts: Collaborative Family Program Development, Peter Fraenkel, PhD, http://www.familyprocess.org/Data/featured_articles/59_ fraenkel.pdf

National Center for Trauma-Informed Care, 66 Canal Center Plaza, Suite 302, Alexandria, VA, 22314. Telephone: 866-254-4819, Fax: 703-548-9517

National Fatherhood Initiative, 20410 Observation Drive, Suite 107, Germantown, MD, 20876. Telephone: 301-948-0599

Nurse-Family Partnership National Service Office, 1900 Grant Street, Suite 400, Denver, CO, 80203. Telephone: 303-327-4240 or 866-864-5226, Email: info@nurse familypartnership.org, http://www.nursefamilypartnership.org/

Rise Magazine: Stories by and for Parents Affected by the Child Welfare System, http://risemagazine.org/index.html

Resources: Family Engagement. (2010, updated 2011). National Resource Center for Permanency and Family Connections (NRCPFC), www.nrcpfc.org

![CWLA logo]

National Blueprint

for Excellence in Child Welfare

IV. Supports and Services

PRINCIPLE

Families, individuals, communities, organizations, and systems protect children from abuse and neglect, and provide an array of supports and services that help children, youth, and their families to accomplish developmental tasks, develop protective factors, and strengthen coping strategies.

At any given time, in any community children, youth, and families may need assistance from a variety of sources: neighbors, friends and family, local faith-based organizations and associations, and the social service, educational, behavioral heath, and health organizations that are designed to improve the well-being of those in need. To build upon the innate resilience of children, youth, families, and communities and to provide meaningful opportunities for personal growth and success, entities must work together with community partners, and must share decisionmaking authority. Together, they must build resources and develop the wherewithal to ensure sustainability.

It is also crucial that communities are healthy environments, in which children, youth, and families can develop and flourish. All entities must work together to prevent and eradicate obstacles to healthy development. Critical issues of poverty, racial and ethnic disparity and disproportionality, violence, and the impact of trauma must be addressed collaboratively as organizations and communities work together to create optimum circumstances for improving outcomes for children, youth, and families.

STANDARDS

COMMUNITY VOICE IN POLICY AND PROGRAM DEVELOPMENT

IV.1. Community members should voice their opinions concerning development of policies and programs that meet the needs of the community, and the families and individuals that live and work in it. (See also *Shared Responsibility and Leadership* on page 22.)

When policymakers, funders, and public and private entities include communities in decisionmaking, supports and services are more likely to meet needs than when community voices are not heeded. When the community's voices are heard, supports and services are culturally responsive and can meet the needs of the children, youth, and families they are designed to serve. (See also *Engagement/Participation* on page 55.)

In an economically challenged environment, with ever-increasing needs of children, youth, and families, there is a moral, ethical, and human imperative to work together to solve problems and make wise decisions about the use of limited resources in ways that community leaders recommend.

Community members should not wait to be invited to the table. They should raise their collective voices; should approach public entities, organizations, and political leaders to make known the community's needs; and advocate for appropriate supports and services.

SAFE AND HEALTHY COMMUNITIES

IV. 2. Every geographic community should strive to create and sustain a safe physical environment, and a culture that promotes making healthy lifestyle choices.

Too many children, youth, and families live in areas and homes where there are risks to safety because of violence and criminal activity, poor maintenance, exposure to toxins, and environmental degradation. Community members should work together to combat all of these risks, and to improve living conditions, health, and safety. (See also *Psychological Safety* on page 18.)

Simultaneously, communities that support unhealthy behaviors threaten too many children, youth, and families. Obesity, overweight, and chronic diseases are at epidemic levels in communities across the United States.[xxiv] Chronic diseases and conditions such as heart disease, stroke, diabetes, cancer, obesity, and arthritis cause suffering and limitations to daily functioning. Preventable health risks such as tobacco use and exposure, substance abuse, insufficient physical activity, and poor nutrition are contributing factors: "The link between social determinants of health, including social, economic, and environmental conditions, and health outcomes is widely recognized in the public health literature. Moreover, it is increasingly understood that inequitable distribution of these conditions across various populations is a significant contributor to persistent and pervasive health disparities." [xxv]

Communities can and should take an active role in improving health and reducing risk factors among community members. Community activity can have a significant effect on the behavior of community members and health risks. For example, researchers have found that mass media campaigns reduce smoking in homes, and that policy changes, such as laws regulating smoking in certain spaces or protecting children from smoke exposure, may also be effective in reducing secondhand smoke exposure. [xxvi]

Community members should collaborate with national, state, local, and tribal entities to support good health and create safe, healthy living environments.

MEETING BASIC NEEDS

IV. 3. Entities and communities should collaborate to ensure that families have access to and eligibility for supports and services that address basic needs, including food, clothing, housing,

employment, financial resources, mental health and substance abuse, education, health care, and transportation.

Communities are important partners in meeting the basic needs of families so that they can successfully care for themselves and their children. Each community should recognize that to be a healthy, happy, productive place to live, individual members must be able to meet their basic needs.

Each community should establish networks to facilitate communication when a particular family has unmet basic needs. Community members should work together so that all families and individuals living and working there know that it is a safe place where people look out for each other. Individual community members should feel responsible for paying attention and noticing when families are unable or struggling to meet their basic needs, and should help access networks to provide support when needed. (See also *Rights of Children* on page 27.)

Children should not be more likely to come to the attention of child protective authorities when they live in one zip code as opposed to another. All communities can be healthy and safe places for children, youth, and families to live, and all communities can meet the basic needs of the children, youth, and families who live in them. All levels of society must work together to counteract and mitigate the long-term effects of poverty and neglect on certain communities. (See also *Disparity and Disproportionality* on page 114.)

IV. 4. When necessary, families should be provided assistance to develop the skills and/or assistance in meeting their children's basic needs, so that children can be safe in their homes.

Parents may be unable to care for their children without assistance for a variety of reasons, including youth or inexperience, income level, substance abuse, accident or illness, disability, mental health, or intergenerational or family patterns.

Children and youth should be protected from unsafe situations. When parents cannot care for their children independently, whenever possible, there should be efforts to provide support and assistance needed for children to remain safely in their homes before consideration of removal. Support and assistance include, but are not limited to: housing, skill-building including coping with stress; obtaining job skills or parenting classes; mentoring programs; parent aides; home visiting; mental health, substance abuse, and domestic violence services, and supervision by a professional, volunteer, or family member.

Parents with disabilities should not be denied a right to parent on the basis of a disability.[xxvii] Parents with disabilities may be eligible for parenting support or assistance through a state or local entity for people with disabilities.

SOCIAL CONNECTIONS

IV. 5. Children, youth, and families should have ample opportunities for safe, positive social connections within their own communities.

Having strong social connections is one characteristic of resilient families.[xxviii] Building social connections helps families and children find support within their own communities. When families are comfortable and connected within their communities, they and their children are more likely to feel safe, which reduces the impact of stress and helps to build resilience.

It is important to help families develop resources in their own communities and to encourage reaching out to friends and neighbors. It is also beneficial to help families to distinguish between supportive resources and those that might threaten family safety or represent barriers to community connectedness.

Research shows that reducing isolation and increasing social connections are keys to reducing stress and increasing family and individual resilience.[xxix]

FOOD AND NUTRITION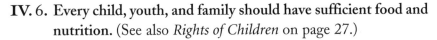

IV. 6. Every child, youth, and family should have sufficient food and nutrition. (See also *Rights of Children* on page 27.)

More than 16 million children under 18 in the United States live in households in which they do not have consistent access to enough nutritious food necessary for a healthy life.[xxx] More than 31 million children in the United States participate in the school lunch program, and more than 12 million participate in the school breakfast program. Food insecurity poses a threat to anyone who experiences it, but is particularly dangerous for children due to their increased vulnerability and the potential for long-term consequences.[xxxi]

Households with low incomes are challenged to find affordable, nutritious food, putting them at risk for chronic disease and obesity.[xxxii]

Each provider should have information about food and nutrition supports and assistance that are available in the community, such as entitlement and other assistance programs, school meals, weekend backpack programs, food pantries, and community meal programs.

Each community should develop sufficient food and nutrition resources and ensure that its children and youth have adequate access to these services. Every community, regardless of income level, should work toward having local access to fresh, healthy, affordable, and culturally appropriate food. Communities that do not have access to fresh foods can explore the development of community gardens, urban greenhouses, and urban farms. They can build support for grassroots efforts to provide healthful, locally grown, fresh food. (See also *Rights of Children* on page 27.)

ACCESS TO HEALTH CARE

IV. 7. Children, youth, and families should have access to health care in their communities, and their health care needs should be met.

Partnerships should be created to ensure that the health care needs of all children, youth, and families are met, including children served in their own homes and those in out-of-home care. Services should include primary, tertiary, and specialty care, including behavioral health and mental health services. Medical providers should be sensitive to the health implications of adverse childhood experiences. [xxxiii]

Each child, youth, and family should have a medical home [xxxiv] [xxxv] that manages and facilitates all aspects of care. Medical care should be delivered or directed by well-trained physicians, who are known to the child or youth and family, and develop a partnership of mutual responsibility and trust with them.

IV. 8. Strategies should be in place to ensure comprehensive health care assessments for all children. Every child should have access to health services to address physical, dental, behavioral health, mental health, emotional, and/or developmental health needs.

Mechanisms for ensuring health care include:

- Inclusion of children, youth, and families in universal health care programs;

- Development of effective collaboration among providers serving children, youth, and families;

- Employment of health care professionals where children and families are served, like child care centers and schools;

- Tracking of health care data;

- Comprehensive health assessments; and

- Centralized and accessible health centers.

There should be mechanisms for ensuring continuity of services when children, youth, and families relocate.

Children who do not have access to health care are at high risk of poor physical and mental health and poor developmental outcomes. Children who are victims of abuse, neglect, and other trauma are at high risk of serious health problems in adulthood.

Parents who do not have access to health care are at higher risk of poor health outcomes, and at high risk of problems with caring for their children.

IV. 9. **Each child and youth should have a comprehensive, accessible, central health record that contains all pertinent information about the child or youth and preserves confidentiality.**

The health record should be maintained according to applicable laws and regulations,[xxxvii] [xxxviii] [xxxix] including accessibility, confidentiality, and portability.

Whenever possible, the record should be maintained by the child or youth's medical home. (See also *Access to Health Care* on page 66.) The child or youth's parent or guardian should keep duplicate information. If the child or youth is in the physical or legal custody of a public agency, the medical record should be maintained by the entity and should be provided to the parent or youth at the time of termination of services.

NORMALIZING NEED FOR SUPPORT

IV. 10. Each entity and community should develop plans for helping to reduce stigma and normalize the need for support and services for the children, youth, and families it serves.

At some point in life, almost every human being needs assistance to cope with challenges, and most people need to seek supports and services. Yet, in spite of this reality, there is stigma attached to needing help that sometimes means children, youth, and families do not seek or accept the assistance they need. It is the responsibility of every person to help shift societal norms and attitudes so that fewer children, youth, and families will be reluctant to engage in supports and services when they need them.

The language of human services should be supportive and positive. All entities and providers should focus on reducing labels, using language to promote recognition of strengths, and building resilience based upon those strengths.

CAREGIVING CHILDREN AND YOUTH

IV. 11. Children and youth who have caregiving responsibilities within their families or households should be provided with appropriate assistance and support.

Children and youth provide significant or substantial caregiving assistance, often on a regular basis, to relatives or household members who need help because of physical or mental illness, disability,[xl] frailty associated with aging, substance misuse, or other conditions. The American Association for Caregiving Youth (AACY)[xli] estimates that there are more than 1.4 million child and youth caregivers in the United States who are between the ages of 8 and 18.

Youth caregivers, especially those living with their care recipients, can experience significantly higher anxiety and depression than their non-caregiving peers. [xlii] Caregiving children and youth are more likely to come from households with lower income, and less likely to live in two parent families. In certain cultures, it may be a cultural norm for children and youth to be caregivers. [xliii] When offering assistance to children and youth caregivers, it is necessary to be aware of cultural norms and expectations.

Communities should take proactive roles to identify the often hidden population of caregiving children and youth, intervene to help them to manage their responsibilities, and support them so they can remain in school and become healthy productive adults.

When family health situations are identified, children and youth should be referred to social work staff. Tutoring, counseling, financial assistance, and food resources are common needs of caregiving children and youth.

When possible, caregiving children and youth should be connected with caregiving peers through support group or club meetings. Online support options may be more appropriate for those who have access to computers. [xliv]

TRAUMA-INFORMED APPROACHES

IV. 12. Each entity should take responsibility for ensuring that all parties providing supports and services are educated about the effects of trauma and the resulting symptoms of traumatic stress, as well as about effective strategies for dealing with it. (See also *Engagement/Participation* on page 48.)

A system with a trauma-informed perspective is one in which each entity:

- Routinely screens for adverse childhood experiences, trauma exposure, and related symptoms; [xiv]

- Uses culturally appropriate assessment and treatment for traumatic stress and associated mental health symptoms;

- Makes resources available to children, youth, families, and providers on trauma exposure, its impact, and treatment;

- Engages in efforts to strengthen the protective factors and the resilience of children, youth, and families impacted by and vulnerable to trauma;

- Addresses parent and caregiver trauma and its impact on the family system;

- Assesses the impact of historical trauma on the child, youth, and family; (See also *Race, Ethnicity and Culture* on page 108.)

- Emphasizes continuity and collaboration of support and service across child-serving systems; and

- Maintains an environment of care for staff that recognizes, minimizes, and addresses secondary traumatic stress, and that increases staff hardiness and resilience. (See also *Workforce* on page 103.)

COLLABORATION

IV. 13. Entities and communities should endeavor to provide a holistic, comprehensive, and integrated experience for children, youth, and families seeking support and receiving services.

Multidisciplinary collaboration offers the best hope of creating multiple, connected points of entry, making it possible for families to access information and supports, utilize services, and avoid falling through the cracks. (See also *Public-Private Collaboration* on page 126.)

There should be structures and processes to coordinate and integrate a child and family's support and services across public agencies and providers. Such structures and processes ensure service continuity and reduce duplication and redundancy. They can also strengthen programs by increasing staff's access to different types of information and expertise, and can help to reduce program costs through joint funding opportunities.

ASSESSMENT AND SERVICE PLANNING

IV. 14. Each entity should have clearly articulated policies and procedures for assessment and service planning that include, at a minimum:

- **Timeframes for completion;**

- **Persons to be included in meetings, and/or consulted by phone or correspondence;**

- **Mechanisms for reassessing and updating plans;**

- **Obtaining necessary acknowledgements, consents and signatures;**

- **Guidelines for confidentiality and information sharing; and**

- **Mechanisms for working with collaborative providers.** (See also *Engagement/Participation* on page 46 and *Race, Ethnicity, and Culture* on page 108.)

While assessment and service planning are not relevant for all services and supports children, youth and families might access (such as accessing the YMCA/YWCA). But when they are, an assessment should be a meaningful process of gathering information, completing needed tests and using valid tools and protocols.

An assessment should never be an empty checklist process. An assessment should gather only as much information as is necessary and should be neither overly intrusive nor cumbersome.

Too often, children, youth, and families have been subjected to numerous assessments collecting the same information across disciplines and providers, with varied results and conflicting recommendations.

Whenever a child, youth, or family is involved with multiple public entities, organizations, and providers, all of them should work together to exchange information, reduce redundancy, and establish a team process. Whenever possible, meetings should be consolidated.

Assessment and service planning should be congruent with each child, youth, and family's culture, and should be completed by staff that are culturally competent and exhibit cultural humility.

GENDER-APPROPRIATE SERVICES

IV. 15. Each entity should ensure that its supports and services are gender-appropriate and take gender differences into consideration.

Everyone should recognize that some gender differences could be attributed to gender discrimination and societal limitations. All entities should continue to work toward full gender equality in education, employment, economic opportunity, and child and youth participation in sports and out-of-school time activities.

At the same time, there should be recognition that there are differences between males and females [xlvi] [xlvii] [xlviii] that affect how they learn, rates of maturation, brain development, emotional experiences, responses to stress, resilience, and tendency toward certain diseases.

Each entity should examine its programs and practices in relation to gender differences to ensure that gender-specific adjustments are implemented as needed.

LEGAL SYSTEM

IV. 16. Courts and other members of the legal system should become a part of the collaborative process to ensure that actions taken are in the best interests of children, protect their rights, and take every possible measure to help them flourish.

Courts play an essential role in balancing the best interests of the child and the rights of families, and ensuring that service providers are accountable and fulfill their responsibilities. By being integrated in local collaborative activities without compromising their objectivity in regard to individual cases, courts and other legal staff can help to drive needed reform.

Statutory requirements and court processes should be revised to move toward less adversarial processes, and to support a flexible continuum of services and legal options that help children, youth and families flourishing.

Whenever possible, guardians *ad litem;* Court-Appointed Special Advocates (CASA); attorneys for children, youth, and families; and legal counsel for public entities should work together to improve the legal system. Judges, administrators, clerks, and other court personnel can assess and recognize areas within their system that can benefit children, youth, and families.[xlix]

Alternative dispute processes and mediation should be available routinely, and all courts and legal staff should be aware of them.

Jurisdictions should explore statutory reform to reduce inter-court conflict. Whenever possible, all cases involving children, youth, and families should be handled by the same court.

Jurisdictional action plans and court rules and procedures should be developed to set standards and protocols that support the children, youth, and family.

Co-training among entities (child and family serving agency staff, community providers, public entities, courts, and legal staff) could help to facilitate change for helping children, youth, and families to achieve positive outcomes.

SOCIAL MEDIA AND TECHNOLOGY

IV. 17. Each entity should have policies and procedures that govern the use of technology and social media by staff, volunteers, and people receiving supports and services.[1]

Technology and social media have helped to cause a metamorphosis in the provision of human services. The availability of instant information (albeit, sometimes inaccurate information) allows people to develop instant expertise in almost any subject. Entities can use the Internet and social media to provide support, education, and access to people they might not be able to reach in person. Entities and communities can use social media to increase public awareness of child and family well-being, the impact of trauma, healthy relationships, and to counteract some of the unhealthy messages of television and social media.

It is essential for each entity to have sound policies and procedures to address technology usage by personnel and children, youth, and families, including such issues as personal use of work-related technology and boundaries between workforce and children, youth, and families.

IV. 18. Parents, youth, employees, and volunteers within each entity should be educated concerning the risks of technology, Internet, and social media use by children and youth, and about appropriate safety protocols. Children, youth, and

**families, and everyone who works with them should have
access to written recommendations and guidelines for
safe usage.**

Researchers are constantly adding to the knowledge base concerning the effects of technology on young brains, the impact
of social media on contemporary life, and the significant
stresses of bombardment in an age of information.

Research suggests that some kinds of exposure to technology may be harmful to children and youth. Cell phone use after
lights-out may be associated with poor mental health, suicidal
feelings, and self-injury in both early and late adolescence.[li]
Background television is distracting to young children, even
when the television programming is meant for adult viewers.[lii]
Students who engage in instant messaging while doing academic work take longer to achieve results.[liii] Children who are
exposed to X-rated sexual material, especially violent material,
are more likely to engage in sexually aggressive behaviors.[liv]

Technology introduces new and significant risks to privacy and confidentiality. Increased use of technology by children and teens exposes them to safety risks due to disclosure
of personal information, online bullying, and targeting by
predators. Thirty-seven percent of teens surveyed report that
they witness online cruelty or meanness sometimes or frequently, and 15% report that they have been victims of online
meanness or cruelty.[lvi]

The Children's Online Privacy Protection Act
(COPPA),[lvii] effective since 2000, was intended to protect
children while they use the Internet, and to place parents in
control of information collected from their young children
online. The efficacy of the intended protection is question-
able, however, because children—many of whom are younger
than the required age—regularly use social media sites without parental permission or knowledge.

The implications of research and patterns of usage are significant for providers of services to children, youth, and families, and for settings such as schools, libraries, out-of-school programs, and any settings in which children and youth might have access to computers.

IV. 19. Each entity should have mechanisms for storing and protecting electronic data that are reviewed and updated to ensure continued efficacy.

The efficacy of digital information allows instant access to information that was incomprehensible just a few years ago. Each entity should have policies and procedures to protect against lapses in security, provide sufficiently for safe data storage that protects against loss, tampering and access by unauthorized persons.

RESOURCES

Allen, W. & Wilson, C. (2012). *The Good Food Revolution: Growing Healthy Food, People and Communities.* New York: Gotham Books.

American Association of Caregiving Youth, Telephone: 800-725-2512, http://www.aacy.org/

Adverse Childhood Experiences Study, http://acestudy.org/home

APHSA Gainful Employment and Independence: A Pathways Policy Brief — August 24, 2012

APHSA Healthier Families, Adults, and Communities: A Pathways Policy Brief — August 24, 2012

CDC (Centers for Disease Control) Essentials for Childhood: Steps to Create Safe, Stable, and Nurturing Relationships (2013), http://www.cdc.gov/violenceprevention/pdf/EFC-01-03-2013-a.pdf

CDC (Centers for Disease Control) Tools for Community Action, http://www.cdc.gov/healthycommunitiesprogram/tools/index.htm#cg

CDC Health Disparities and Inequalities Report — United States, 2011, http:// www.cdc.gov/mmwr/pdf/other/su6001.pdf

GrandFacts: Data, Interpretation, and Implications for Caregivers (2009). Washington, DC: Generations United.

Lietz, C. A. (2007). Uncovering Stories of Family Resilience: A Mixed Methods Study of Resilient Families, Part 2. *Families in Society, 88*(1), 147-155.

National Child Traumatic Stress Network. (2012). *Creating Trauma-Informed Systems,* http://www.nctsn.org/resources/topics/creating-trauma-informed-systems.

Social Media for Child Welfare Resource Guide (2012). National Resource Center for Child Welfare Data & Technology, http://www.nrccwdt.org/2012/09/the-social-media-for-child-welfare-resource-guide/

Supplemental Nutrition Assistance Program (SNAP) Community Characteristics Interactive Map, http://www.fns.usda.gov/ora/SNAPCharacteristics/default.htm

USDA Center for Nutrition Policy and Promotion, http://www.cnpp.usda.gov/

NATIONAL BLUEPRINT

FOR EXCELLENCE IN CHILD WELFARE

V. Quality Improvement

Supports and services are designed and implemented based on evidence and knowledge; data collection is focused on measuring outcomes and achieving success; continuous quality improvement is emphasized and supported; and innovative practices and programs are encouraged.

Achieving an ambitious vision for children and youth is an extraordinarily momentous task, with no "cookbook" or easy shortcuts that staff can take for granted. Instead, successful organizations use all the evidence available to them to make good judgments up front—and then constantly collect information to find out how they are doing and how they might need to fine-tune their approaches. Evidence about "learning organizations" from many fields suggests that it is crucial to have good data of many kinds: quantitative; qualitative; feedback from youth, families, and staff; information about the quality of the day-to-day work and processes; and information about immediate and longer-term outcomes. It is also crucial to have an environment that supports learning, ongoing change, and creativity. Curiosity, and personal involvement in looking at what the data show, need to flow both from the top down—with regular involvement by top leadership—and from the bottom up, with individuals working directly with children and families. Supervisors must also be supported to review and learn more about the quality of their own work and their peers' work.

"Quality Improvement" programs can be complex, and sometimes overwhelm staff and constituencies with surveys, data, and jargon. However, at their core, the purpose of quality improvement programs is very simple: to make things better.

A good quality improvement program has no beginning and no end; it functions continuously like a well-oiled machine. It determines to what extent the entity is accomplishing what it intends to accomplish. It establishes anticipated outcomes. It measures its performance against an established yardstick. It seeks and finds things that can be improved; identifies how they can be improved; explains the reasons that alternatives are indicated; demonstrates that, in fact, the change is beneficial; and, if it is not beneficial, makes an alternative change.

A successful quality improvement model requires a structure for collecting and reviewing data, a culture and climate conducive to supporting positive change, and managers and personnel who are committed to doing the best work they can do.

Every entity should implement a quality improvement model— whether organized as a separate program, built into the regular operational structure at all levels, or both. Its nature may differ according to the entity's size, structure, statutory and mandated accountability, and other variables, but the focus should always be the same: to constantly gather information about the quality and outcomes of work; to use that information to learn about strengths and weaknesses, as well as other unanticipated trends or consequences; and to use the learning to improve the entity's policies, programs, structures, day-to-day work processes, and short-term and lifelong outcomes for children, youth, and families.

STANDARDS

COMPONENTS OF QUALITY IMPROVEMENT PROGRAMS

V.1. Each entity should have a quality improvement program that has the following components:

- Clearly articulated vision, values, and mission that define the purpose and direction of the entity and set the parameters for its accomplishments;

- Plans for achieving the entity's purpose and direction;

- Structure and mechanisms for gathering quantitative and qualitative information about work processes, quality, and outcomes;

- Effective and ongoing processes for examining information, sharing information with people who need it, evaluating information, and making decisions based upon it;

- Processes for making change;

- Processes for evaluating the effects of change; and

- Multiple opportunities and mechanism for reporting results, including regular reporting on key measures and special reporting on emerging or urgent issues.

These generic requirements can be applied to any public entity, any organization or provider, any setting, any size staff, and even to an individual practitioner. While a quality improvement description might be much more detailed and sophisticated in a large organization, these simple requirements are intended to capture the basic, universal elements of quality improvement programs.

POSITIVE CULTURE AND CLIMATE

V.2. Within each entity, everyone should be responsible for creating and sustaining a culture and climate in which accountability, communication, responsiveness, and commitment to improvement are valued and rewarded. (See also *Workforce* on page 99.)

The notion of personal responsibility for quality improvement should be integrated into strategic plans, operating policies and procedures, staff evaluation processes, and customer/consumer satisfaction surveys.

Evidence about learning organizations indicates that the broad culture is crucial. For example, health care organizations that have successfully improved safety outcomes and reduced errors (such as hospitals that have reduced medication errors) have focused on ensuring a culture in which everyone understands and adopts the vision and sees it as their personal responsibility—while also feeling supported and safe in acknowledging their own missteps or areas for improvement. Without a shared culture of responsibility for the goals, paired with a shared feeling of safety that allows for honest reporting and use of data, it is hard for organizations to improve.

Top leadership must model and support such a culture for it to take hold. At all levels, managers and supervisors should embody the culture in their own work and teach it to those they supervise. Staff should see how their day-to-day work fits into the culture. Often, organizations working toward such a culture identify mixed messages that are hindering the development of a clear and consistent culture. Effective learning organizations treat the evidence of such mixed messages as a valuable data point and work to change spoken and unspoken policy so that all of the messages are consistent.

Although no organization can guarantee that everyone will be of the same mind regarding responsibility, once an organization establishes that accountability, communication, responsiveness, and commitment to improvement are valued, then everyone is responsible for helping to implement that expectation. Each person must take personal responsibility for these attributes of quality—in personal performance, the work of groups and units, and the entity as a whole.

TRANSPARENCY

V.3. **To assure accountability, build trust in the community, and contribute to collaborative relationships, each entity's quality**

improvement process should be transparent to children, youth, and families; other stakeholders; and the general public.

A transparent quality improvement program demonstrates accountability and adds credibility to an entity's claim that it successfully accomplishes its goals. Transparency also helps build evidence to support or refute theories and constructs, contributes to practice knowledge bases, and leads to program innovation and further responsiveness to the needs of children, youth, families, and communities. (See also *Engagement/ Participation* on page 50 and *Shared Responsibility* and *Leadership* on page 42.)

V.4. Qualitative and quantitative data gathered by organizations and public entities should be available for review by stakeholders.

Entities working with families that are vulnerable often feel that they face unique obstacles to transparency, including the confidentiality of information and the intense public reaction, which can make it uncomfortable to share negative information. However, entities that do the hard work to identify measures and standards, share them regularly without violating confidentiality, and then share the updates whether good or bad news, often find that they have built trust that helps them weather difficult situations.

SOLICITING AND CONSIDERING FEEDBACK

V.5. Each entity should have mechanisms for soliciting and considering feedback—from children, youth, families, partners, collaborators, other stakeholders, and community members—that are appropriate to its size and the scope of its mission.

Stakeholder feedback is indispensable to quality improvement in any organization. Assessment of the efficacy of the work is not possible without consideration of the opinions of the people affected by the work. The opinions of children, youth, and families who have participated in or are receiving the supports and services should be valued and considered, as should the opinions of other community stakeholders.

An environment that has cultivated a healthy culture and climate has a variety of formal and informal mechanisms for receiving and welcoming feedback. Surveys, focus groups, suggestion boxes, performance evaluations, and complaint procedures are examples of formal mechanisms. Informal mechanisms—including open-door policies, "drop-in" times or events, and routine questions at the end of each meeting, such as, "Are there any suggestions?"—help to deliver a consistent message that there is a sincere desire to involve stakeholders in improving quality and outcomes. (See also *Making Improvements* on page 90 and *Engagement/Participation* on page 56.)

It is crucial not to omit feedback from populations that are particularly challenging to reach as they may have the most important information. For example, public child welfare agencies have successfully surveyed birth families to understand their circumstances and perspectives.

MEANINGFUL DATA

V.6. Each entity should collect meaningful data to support its ability to make decisions; improve proactively; and help children, youth, and families to achieve identified outcomes.

Many kinds of data are crucial to understanding whether an entity is providing the services it intends to provide, at the level of quality it means to offer, and whether it is accomplishing the outcomes it desires. Quantitative data about both process and outcomes—for example, about the timeliness of assessments or medical appointments, or the percentage of children who are reading at grade level—offer the opportunity to scan performance across a large sample relatively frequently. When such data highlight critical issues, or if quantitative data do not exist, it can be useful to look more in-depth at a smaller sample, using both quantitative and qualitative methods. Interviews with service recipients and results of satisfaction surveys can provide qualitative data.

People in all parts and at all levels of the organization should have access to the data they need. In some organizations, a team process for identifying key data, collecting it, and mining it for lessons may be the best approach.

As data collection approaches are developed and improved, the purpose should be clear to everyone involved in providing it, collecting it, and maintaining it. In an organization with a culture of learning, data are used primarily to identify strengths and weaknesses, areas in which performance is on track or off track, and opportunities for improvement. Data should not be used to focus on blaming.

While entities often have to start with data that are not perfect for the goals they have in mind, data collection should itself be subject to continuous improvement—with improved measures and approaches to data collection a built-in part of the process. Researchers in many different organizations have found that effective learning organizations typically start with the data they have, but work steadily toward improving data quality as they get further on their trajectory toward continuous improvement. (See also *Engagement/Participation* on page 56 and *Workforce* on page 94.)

EVIDENCE-BASED PROGRAMS AND PRACTICES

V. 7. **Entities should develop and implement only those programs and practices that are based upon the best available evidence.**

Children, youth, and families need and deserve effective services. Providers and funders of supports and services should be accountable to service users and communities regarding the effectiveness and efficiency of services provided. Each entity has an obligation to use practices for which there is evidence of effectiveness, or, when such evidence is lacking, to test for effectiveness and accumulate evidence.

Those aspiring to excellence have an obligation to be familiar with the current research and science regarding the efficacy of the practices and programs they use.

Programs and practices should be developed and selected after consideration of issues to be addressed, the population served, the workforce available, and the community in which the services is to be delivered.

Evidence-based[lviii] programs and practices—those supported by empirical evidence—are preferred if they are deemed a good fit for the target problem, the clients served, the resources available, the workforce delivering them, and the community's values and culture. An "evidence-based" label, however, is not a guarantee of quality, nor does it ensure that the particular program or approach is appropriate for the application under consideration or for populations being served.

There are many resources for identifying the kind of evidence that supports a program or practice and the extent to which it is a fit for the intended use. Clearinghouses[lix] that have categorized models and practices as evidence-based, evidence-informed, promising, emerging, or practice-based may be helpful to those reviewing and selecting program and practice options.

PRACTICE-BASED EVIDENCE

V. 8. **Practitioners and researchers should work together effectively to improve knowledge of what works in helping children, youth, and families to flourish.**[lx]

Programs and practices should be implemented consistently to assure fidelity to models and to build evidence of their effectiveness. Many practitioners and researchers argue, however, that too much insistence on scientific evidence can cause oversight of compelling, practice-based evidence. In order to serve children, youth, and families well, both evidence-based practice and practice-based evidence (see *Definitions*) are required.[lxi] However, sometimes there is not adequate evidence regarding a specific population or a planned implementation. When alterations and adaptations to tested models are needed, the models' developers should be consulted. The adaptation or new application can be added to practice-based evidence concerning the efficacy of the model.

Practice-based evidence also emerges from observations of children, youth, and families who are flourishing.

MEASURING OUTCOMES

V.9. Outcome measures should reflect both aspirations and achievable impact on supports and services for children, youth, and families.

The ultimate intent of programs, practices, and services is to improve the well-being of children, youth, families in all life domains so that they will flourish.[lxii] Children, youth, and families should share their aspirations. Their desires should be central to determining the outcomes, and outcome measures utilized. (See also *Engagement/Participation* on page 46)

It is essential that each collaborating partner establishes clearly articulated, measurable outcomes based on their role in supporting and serving children, youth, families, and communities. Outcomes and process indicators should also be established collaboratively for the system as a whole, drawing on data from each respective partner. It is important that outcomes for children, youth, and families support efforts so that children and youth can flourish at individual and community levels.

Outcomes should be regularly reviewed to assess progress and promote evidence-informed decisionmaking.

With established meaningful outcomes, entities can measure the impact of services to children, youth, families, and communities. When able to measure impact, entities know whether they are assisting children, youth, or families in reaching success in their lives.

Effective outcome measures will provide clear indications of success and of the need for alternative approaches and interventions when outcomes are not achieved.

BENCHMARKS

V. 10. Each entity should establish benchmarks for all program areas and systems functions.

Benchmarks must be set in the context of an entity's mission, vision, and values, and with consideration for the roles and responsibilities of the organization or provider in relation to other partners.

Quality improvement processes should identify how benchmarks are used, and how striving to meet them is expected to drive changes that will improve outcomes for children, youth, and families.

Benchmarks should be based on evidence, and should be chosen carefully. They should not be arbitrary. Benchmarks should not be confused with goals, outcomes, or outcome measures.

Benchmarks that are included in performance-based contracting should be reasonable and should be identified jointly by funders, contractors, and any additional partners. Benchmarks established within contracts should be linked to systemic benchmarks and to system-wide continuous quality improvement processes.

MAKING IMPROVEMENTS

V. 11. When evidence indicates that performance is not meeting expectations, the entity should take action to make improvements that are informed by evidence.

Each entity should review and analyze its data regularly to determine how work is progressing, what opportunities for improvement there are, and what changes should be made to progress toward established outcomes.

Quality improvement programs, when used correctly, inspire proactive solutions and reduce the number and frequency of reactive solutions.

Objective assessment and honest appraisal lead to understanding what is working, what should be improved, and how it can be improved. A successful quality improvement program can demonstrate positive change as a result of its quality improvement process. (See also *Shared Responsibility and Leadership* on page 39.)

RESEARCH

V. 12. Organizations should collaborate with universities and other entities conducting research. Universities and other researchers should disseminate research findings widely to contribute to research to practice applications.

Entities should operate quality improvement initiatives or programs and document their work to produce data regarding the effectiveness of supports and services provided. Data produced should be used to inform program and service improvements at organizational levels, systems levels, and across systems.

Published results of single-case, small-group, utilization reviews, and larger studies can add to the knowledge base of what works and what does not.

Researchers and entities should exchange information about availability of quality improvement data and other data sets. Researchers should make a commitment to collaborate with entities in affordable ways and to disseminate findings that will guide research-to-practice efforts. Conversely, quality improvement data from entities and organizations should be available to help researchers to determine areas in need of study and evidence.

All use of data should adhere to applicable law and guidelines concerning human subjects and confidentiality.

RESOURCES

Blueprints for Violence Prevention, a project of the Center for the Study and Prevention of Violence at the University of Colorado, http://www.colorado.edu/cspv/blueprints/

California Evidence-Based Clearinghouse, www.cachildwelfareclearinghouse.org

CARF International (Commission on Accreditation of Rehabilitation Facilities), http://www.carf.org/home

Child Welfare Information Gateway – Child Welfare Practice Improvement, http://www.childwelfare.gov/management/practice_improvement/

Child Welfare Information Gateway – Logic Models, http://www.childwelfare.gov/management/effectiveness/logic_model.cfm

COA 8th Edition Performance and Quality Improvement (note that there are differences between the public and private editions), http://www.coastandards.org/standards.php?navView=private&section_id=157, http://www.coastandards.org/standards.php?navView=public&section_id=158

The Annie E. Casey Foundation and The Center for the Study of Social Policy. (2011). *Counting is Not Enough: Investing in Qualitative Case Reviews for Practice Improvement in Child Welfare.* Baltimore, MD: Author.

Farley, C., & Polin, M. (2012). *Collective Ideas to Collective Impact: A Guide to Data Collaboration in Communities.* Austin, TX: NFocus Solutions. Retrieved from http://www.nfocus.com/company/collective-ideas-to-collective-impact.

Georgetown University Center for Child and Human Development – Data Corner, http://www.gucchdgeorgetown.net/data/

Lee, B. R. & Curtis McMillen, J. (2008). Measuring quality in residential treatment for children and youth. *Residential Treatment For Children & Youth, 24*(1), 1-17. Retrieved from http://www.informaworld.com/smpp/title~db=all~content= t792306958~tab=issueslist~branches=24 - v24.

Morris, J. A., Day, S., & Schoenwald, S.K. (2010). *Turning Knowledge Into Practice: A Manual for Human Service Administrators and Practitioners about Understanding and Implementing Evidence-Based Practices (2nd Edition).* Technical Assistance Collaborative.

National Child Traumatic Stress Network (NCTSN), www.nctsn.org

Supporting Evidence Based Home Visiting, http://supportingebhv.org/resources/ researching-home-visiting

Yeager, J. & Saggese, M.L. (2008). Making Your Agency Outcome Informed: A Guide to Overcoming Human Resistance to Change. *Families In Society, 89*(1) 9–18.

U.S. Department of Health and Human Services Home Visiting Evidence of Effectiveness (HomVEE), http://www.acf.hhs.gov/programs/opre/other_resrch/ home_visiting/index.html.

U.S. Office of Juvenile Justice and Delinquency Prevention (OJJDP) Model Programmes Guide, http://www.ojjdp.gov/mpg/

U.S. Office of Juvenile Justice and Delinquency Prevention (OJJDP) Children Exposed to Violence Evidence-Based Guide, http://www.safestartcenter.org/pdf/ Evidence-Based-Practices-Matrix_2011.pdf

U.S. Substance Abuse and Mental Health Administration SAMHSA National Registry of Evidence-Based Programs and Practices (NREPP), http://nrepp. samhsa.gov/

CWLA
NATIONAL BLUEPRINT

FOR EXCELLENCE IN CHILD WELFARE

VI. Workforce

PRINCIPLE

The workforce consists of competent skilled people with a variety of experiences and representing varied disciplines. They are committed to high-quality service delivery and are provided with the training, tools, resources, and support necessary to perform their roles effectively.

Traditionally, the child welfare "workforce" has included people employed by public child welfare agencies and staff working for contracted providers and partner organizations. In the context of the CWLA National Blueprint, "workforce" is considered to be broader. The workforce includes all persons in paid positions of any kind—whether they receive salaries, wages, or stipends—who are engaged in any aspect of service or support to children, youth, and families. The workforce also includes unpaid volunteers and interns working in organizations providing supports and services. The workforce goes beyond people who think of themselves as child welfare. It includes anyone whose efforts contribute to the well-being of children and youth in some way.

With that broad definition, the workforce includes individuals who, while they do not view themselves as child welfare staff, are nonetheless in positions instrumental to moving society toward the CWLA National Blueprint's articulated vision that "all children will grow up safely, in loving families and supportive communities, with everything they need to flourish—and with connections to their culture, ethnicity, race, and language." (See also *Vision* on page 21.) A boxing or gymnastics coach, a scout leader, a classroom teacher, a mentor, a medical professional, a family court judge, a child care center director, and a policeman are all as much a part of the workforce as are the social workers, supervisors, managers, attorneys, mental health professionals and guardians *ad litem* typically identified among child welfare staff.

The workforce must include people in a broad range of disciplines, in addition to social work, who represent a range of personal experiences, including experience with services and supports. (See also

Shared Responsibility and Leadership on page 40.) Every individual must be committed to high-quality supports and services, whether or not that person is actually providing supports and services. (See also *Quality Improvement* on page 80.)

The Standards that follow are intended to be a reference for any and all public agencies; individual and organizational contractors and vendors; and communities and organizations that provide supports and services to address the needs of children, youth, and their families.

STANDARDS

LEADERSHIP (See also *Shared Responsibility and Leadership* on page 40)

VI.1. **Entities at national, state, and local levels should have qualified and visionary leaders who are equipped to transform the broader community response to the changing needs of children, youth, and families within their communities.**

To progress toward having communities and environments in which each child and youth can flourish, the way they work together, how they collaborate, and how they practice must be adapted based on growing bodies of knowledge across disciplines and areas of expertise. Changing practice requires qualified and visionary leaders.

To assure that individuals who fill leadership positions have the necessary knowledge and competencies to lead, each entity should establish criteria for its own leaders. Having established those criteria, each entity should help to build the necessary knowledge, skills, and abilities among its workforce to prepare them for future leadership roles.

VI.2. **Organizational leaders should have the skills, knowledge, and ability to facilitate good governance, help the organization**

focus on its mission, strive toward excellence, develop plans, and create and adhere to appropriate systems to help children, youth, and families.

Within the context of shared leadership among community, family, and other entities, it should be apparent that each entity needs competent leaders with characteristics that are appropriate to meet that entity's needs. (See also *Shared Responsibility and Leadership* on page 38 and *Governance and Capacity* on page 42.)

WORKFORCE DEVELOPMENT

VI.3. Orientation and training programs, and continuing education, whether at the academic or provider level, should be evidence-informed, competency-based, and should include, at a minimum, the following topics:

- Children's rights

- Family and youth engagement strategies

- Familial rights and responsibilities

- The effects of trauma on children, youth, and families

- Child, youth, and adult development

- Communication and collaboration

- Community partnerships

- Appropriate boundaries and prevention of sexual exploitation

- Cultural competence and cultural humility

- Policies and procedures

  Relevant law and regulation

- Topics relevant to the specific position

- Relevant evidence-informed programs and practices

- Self-care and stress management

- Effects of secondary traumatic stress

Each employer should provide orientation to each new employee and volunteer prior to the person working directly with children, youth, and families.

The skills/competencies that training and education are intended to develop should be clear and well-defined. There should be mechanisms for assessing the extent to which a training or education program does, in fact, help the person to develop the intended competency.

Job shadowing is a recommended training technique for use with new employees and volunteers, as well as for people considering promotional opportunities.[lxiii]

Training and continuing education may be offered in-house, externally, or in combination. Entities should consider cross-training to facilitate collaboration and to improve efficiency and cost-saving.

Providers, families, youth, communities, and educational institutions should work together to ensure that curricula are current, accurate, and evidence-informed.

EXPERIENCE AS A SERVICE RECIPIENT

VI.4. Each entity should be committed to including people with experience as service recipients among its employees, volunteers, board members, and advisory groups.

Each entity should encourage youth and families to apply for positions for which they are qualified, and should emphasize that their experiences are considered to be valuable assets. Entities should offer supports and incentives for youth and parents to be involved. When the voices of youth and families are truly valued, they are not expected to volunteer.

Entities should have a formal process to celebrate when parents and youth transition from receiving supports and services to holding paid positions.

People with experience as service recipients should not be locked into positions with limited options for growth and advancement. Entities should have career ladders so that they can move beyond entry level positions. Youth and families need opportunities to develop the professional skills vital to augmenting their experience as service recipients. There should be opportunities them to take courses, enter degree programs, and complete them successfully so that they become qualified for supervisory and management positions that require advanced degrees.

PROFESSIONAL DEVELOPMENT

VI.5. Parents, youth, families, and communities should be part of the development of educational and training programs, and should be involved in the delivery of workforce orientation and training. (See also *Engagement/Participation* on page 52 and *Shared Responsibility and Leadership* on page 39.)

Parents and youth who have experience as service recipients should participate as trainers or co-trainers of staff and Board members.

VI.6. Each employee and volunteer should have education and experience appropriate to their position.

PERFORMANCE EVALUATION

VI.7. The performance of each employee and volunteer should be evaluated at least annually.

Each provider should develop a systematic approach to evaluation that appraises actual performance in relation to stated goals. Goals should be stated clearly and should be measureable. Evaluation should include assessment of the person's training and continuing education needs, and adherence to the entity's training requirements. The evaluation should address the individual's engagement with children, youth, and families, as appropriate for the person's position. The evaluation should establish objectives and assessment criteria for future performance.

POSITIVE CULTURE AND CLIMATE

VI.8. Each employer should cultivate a culture and climate within which accountability, trust, and communication are the norm among all staff, volunteers, and service recipients. (See also *Quality Improvement* on page 82.)

Every organization, regardless of its size, has an organizational culture: the collection of beliefs, values, and norms that govern the behavior of people within the organization. Employees who understand and embrace their organization's culture are most likely to perform well, demonstrate fidelity to the organization's mission, and work well with supervisors and managers. The climate is determined by the feelings and attitudes of the people working there. In general, a healthy organizational climate encourages people to respect each other, appreciate and recognize good work, value learning, think creatively, and be supportive, as well as to help children, youth, and families achieve positive outcomes. [lxiv]

Employees and volunteers in organizations with positive cultures and climates experience reduced conflict, greater job satisfaction, less burnout, greater capacity to manage stress, and are more committed to excellence than their counterparts in other organizations.

Organizations of all sizes can benefit from assessing culture and climate, and from making changes to improve both.

WORKLOAD

VI.9.   There should be assurance that each person's workload is reasonable and allows the employee to perform the required duties. At a minimum, there should be adherence to workload criteria recommended by licensing authorities, the requirements of the specific evidence-based program, and/or accrediting bodies, whenever applicable.

VI.10. Each employer should develop and maintain a workforce of sufficient size to make possible the achievement of identified outcomes for the persons served. (See also *Funding and Resources* on page 121.)

VI.11. Each employer should have a system appropriate to its size and function for evaluating the effectiveness of its workforce and the efficacy of each person's workload.

Each employer should be committed to maintaining all positions that are necessary for adhering to sound practice. When changes in workforce size are necessary, providers should ensure that they do not impact the safety and well-being of children and youth. (See also *Funding and Resources* on page 121.)

Workforce stability is crucial to good outcomes for children, youth, and families, and workforce stability is largely dependent upon ensuring that individuals have adequate supervision and support.

SUPERVISION

VI. 12. **Each employee and volunteer should have and report to a supervisor who has the skills, knowledge, and ability to provide guidance appropriate for the individual's needs, position, and responsibilities.**

Each entity should establish and adhere to baseline expectations for the provision of supervision to each individual. Supervision models may include group, individual, or a combination and should be regularly scheduled. There should be sufficient flexibility in the supervision model to adjust the frequency, duration, and intensity of supervision according to particular performance and needs of the individual, crisis or emergency situations, and other variables.

Supervisors should have received supervisory training, and should demonstrate competence.

A clear mission; high-quality supports and services; and greatest achievement of positive outcomes for children, youth, and families will be achieved only with supervisors who are adequately trained and coached, and who can put the entity's concepts into operation. An entity's effectiveness is achieved in the interaction between supervisors and their staff. [lxv]

There should be clear and measurable performance criteria and workforce appraisal methods that are understood by supervisors and their supervisees.

Quality supervision is pivotal in developing a culture that acknowledges and responds appropriately to the risk of secondary traumatic stress. (See also *Secondary Traumatic Stress and Burnout* on page 103.)

CONTINUOUS LEARNING

VI.13. Each employer should have a plan for furthering the professional growth and development of employees and volunteers, with an eye toward continuous learning and career advancement. (See also *Quality Improvement* on page 80 and *Youth and Family Involvement* on page 49.)

VI.14. Each person should have opportunities to engage in formal and informal learning, on the job, through continuing education, coaching or mentoring, and through collaboration with peers.

Each individual, whether providing direct service, supervising, or managing should continue to grow and learn. It is the responsibility of each community, provider, and public entity to promote such continued learning, and to make it an essential expectation of job performance. People who are excited about learning and enriching their own lives are best able to enrich the lives of those around them—whether peers, clients, supervisors, or supervisees.

As needed, individuals should have access to technical assistance, coaching or mentoring and experiential learning. Alternative approaches to on the job learning promote expansion of knowledge and excitement about continued professional growth.

Learning opportunities should be plentiful, and varied to match the needs of adult learners and the spectrum of learning styles. Supervisors should be familiar with available internal and external learning opportunities, and should assist supervisees in accessing core learning and continuing education that is responsive to needs and stimulates growth.

In-service learning topics should not be stagnant. New topics should be introduced, based upon changing needs and applicable current best practices. Each person's training objectives should be individualized, based upon experience, performance, previous learning, evaluation, and supervision.

Staff should use and apply new skills and knowledge as soon as practical, and should be evaluated based on objectives of a course, training, or on-the-job professional development. Learning organization and transfer of learning concepts should be apparent in each entity. (See also *Professional Development* on page 98.)

SECONDARY TRAUMATIC STRESS AND BURNOUT

VI.15. Each employer should have mechanisms for encouraging and supporting staff self-care, engaging in appropriate prevention and wellness activities, and learning stress-management strategies. (See also *Workforce Development* on page 96.)

VI.16. Each employer should recognize the potential for its employees to be exposed to many different forms of trauma and to secondary traumatic stress. The employer should have plans for responding appropriately to crises and minimizing the effects of secondary traumatic stress.

Working with children, youth, and families that have been affected by abuse, neglect, violence, disasters (manmade or natural) and other kinds of trauma has a profound impact on members of the workforce. Left unattended, it has negative consequences on individual performance, attrition, organizational climate, and the capacity to help children, youth, and families.

Given the prevalence of children, youth, and families that experience some type of trauma at some point in their life and the potential resulting traumatic stress symptoms, each entity should acknowledge the potential for its staff to experience secondary traumatic stress, encouraging ongoing and open discussion of secondary traumatic stress among the workforce and providing the infrastructure to address it.

All personnel should be aware of and understand the signs and behaviors associated with secondary traumatic stress and burnout. All staff should know their emotional limitations and should be encouraged to discuss issues that may impact them personally. Staff that may be experiencing these symptoms should be able to rely on their employer to support them, should have access to intervention and treatment when needed, and should be assured that seeking assistance will not result in judgment or stigma.

Entities with the following characteristics are best able to address the risks of secondary traumatic stress:[lxvii]

- Education and training

- Supervision and consultation

- Safe and pleasant physical setting

- Reasonable/balanced workload

- Adequate coverage and back-up

- Caring and supportive culture

- Opportunities for peer support

- Protocol for debriefing when needed

- Access to quality mental health coverage and employee assistance program (EAP) programs

Addressing secondary traumatic stress is an organizational and personal responsibility, which should be a priority for every entity. (See also *Quality Improvement* on page 81 and *Shared Responsibility and Leadership* on page 41.)

RESOURCES

Alarcon, G.M. (2011). A meta-analysis of burnout with job demands, resources, and attitudes. *Journal of Vocational Behavior, 79* (2), 549–562.

Anderson, G., and Zlotnik, J.L. (Eds.). (2009). Strengthening the Child Welfare Workforce: Promoting Recruitment and Retention [special issue]. *Child Welfare, 88*(5).

Glisson, C., Dukes, D., & Green, P. (2006). The effects of the ARC organizational intervention on caseworker turnover, climate, and culture in children's service systems. *Child Abuse & Neglect, 20*, 855–880.

ACS-NYU Children's Trauma Institute. (2012). Addressing Secondary Traumatic Stress Among Child Welfare Staff: A Practice Brief.

The Children's Bureau Training and Technical Assistance (T/TA) Network: Ten Years of Workforce and Leadership Development Initiatives, Training and Technical Assistance Activities, and Related Products: A Resource Guide, 2000-2010. National Child Welfare Workforce Institute, 2010

National Child Welfare Workforce Institute, www.ncwwi.org

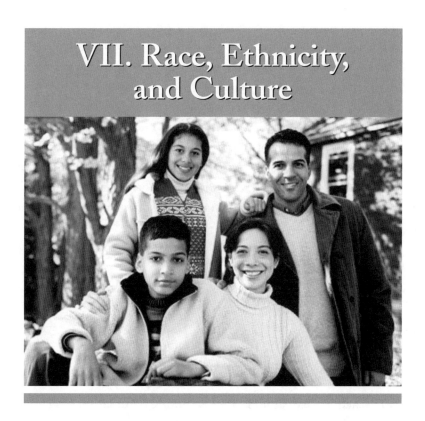

CWLA
NATIONAL BLUEPRINT
FOR EXCELLENCE IN CHILD WELFARE

VII. Race, Ethnicity, and Culture

PRINCIPLE

Individuals, families, communities, organizations, and systems work together to understand, and promote equality, cultural humility, and strong racial, cultural, and ethnic identity, while showing consideration for individual differences and respecting the sovereign rights of tribes.

E veryone working with children, youth, and families must have sincere respect for and commitment to human dignity and human rights issues related to race, ethnicity, and culture. (See also *Rights of Children* on page 25 and *Engagement/Participation* on page 45.)

When cultures and traditions are unfamiliar, all individuals and entities should be willing to learn, and must have resources to help them understand values and norms.

Everyone should interact with others with cultural humility, that is, an understanding that customs, values, and social norms of one culture may be entirely unfamiliar and, perhaps, unacceptable in another culture. Individuals and groups must not make assumptions, and must not impose their own beliefs and norms on other individuals and groups. They must be willing to ask questions and genuinely listen to answers.

Everyone should be committed to respecting and upholding the sovereign rights of tribes.

STANDARDS

NONDISCRIMINATION

VII.1. Each entity should have a nondiscrimination policy that conforms to applicable law and to the Rights of Children section of the CWLA National Blueprint. (See also *Rights of Children* on page 26)

Nondiscrimination requirements vary among federal, state, and local jurisdictions. Some nondiscrimination requirements are guaranteed and protected by the U.S. Constitution and federal laws enacted by Congress, such as the Civil Rights Act of 1964[ixix] and the Americans with Disabilities Act of 1990 as amended in 2008.[lxx] Certain federal nondiscrimination requirements proceed from other federal laws, such as the Equal Employment Opportunity Act.[lxxi] Some jurisdictions have more stringent nondiscrimination requirements, for example, prohibiting discrimination on the basis of citizenship, while other jurisdictions condone such discrimination. In some jurisdictions, individuals and groups may be protected from discrimination in some realms, for example, lending and housing, but not in others such as education and receipt of nonemergency medical services. In some jurisdictions, licensing regulations mandate nondiscrimination requirements for licensed providers that may be more specific than those in statute, for example, licensing regulations may prohibit discrimination on the basis of sexual orientation and marital status.[lxxii]

The CWLA National Blueprint recommends nondiscrimination policies that may be broader than legal requirements when they are felt to be in the best interest of child well-being, and encourages all entities and jurisdictions to work toward the adoption of policies that are inclusive and protect all those served from discrimination. Each entity must determine the applicability of relevant laws, and the entities should work together to protect all children, youth, and families from discrimination on the basis of race, color, age, disability, gender, familial status, religion, sexual orientation, gender identity, genetic information, language, religion, national, ethnic or social origin, political beliefs, or citizenship.

Each entity should post its nondiscrimination statement in locations where the statement may be seen and read. If people in the community and/or people receiving support and services speak languages other than English, the statement should be posted in those other languages.

Communities must ensure that all residents can receive appropriate supports and services, regardless of any limitations that might be imposed due to religious beliefs, language capacity, accessibility of buildings or any other limitations. If there are such limitations among service providers, the community should compensate by assuring that there are reasonable and appropriate services available from another provider. Where such resources do not yet exist, the community should work toward developing them.

All individuals and entities should recognize the role that historical discrimination and historical trauma can play in the current experience of children, youth, and families, whether or not they have had these experiences themselves. (See also *Engagement/Participation* on page 48, *Trauma-Informed Approaches* on page 69, and *Workforce* on page 103.)

INDIGENOUS NATIONS

VII.2. In all relations with indigenous nations, each entity should adhere to the principles of self-determination, holistic approaches, elimination of structural risk, respect for culture and language, and nondiscrimination.[lxxiii]

All entities should acknowledge and affirm the sovereign rights of tribes, and the moral authority of indigenous peoples' governments to make decisions about their children. Having recognized that indigenous peoples are in the best position to make decisions about indigenous children and youth, governments, systems, tribes, organizations, and providers should move forward together, in a respectful way, to achieve better outcomes for indigenous children, youth, and families.

Work should be guided by recognition that truth and reconciliation are essential to healing of Indigenous nations.

The key values—Self Determination, Culture and Language, Holistic Approach, Structural Interventions, and Nondiscrimination—are essential to successful supports and services for indigenous children, youth, and families, and should guide relationships between indigenous and non-indigenous people in the workforce.

INDIAN CHILD WELFARE

VII.3. Each entity should minimize cultural disruption and alienation for American Indian/Alaska Native children, youth, and families, use active efforts to prevent unnecessary removal from their families, and understand the Indian Child Welfare Act (ICWA), and how it applies to their work with children, youth, and families.

It is essential that supports and services are culturally relevant to the unique needs of tribal and urban American Indian/Alaska Native families, and that they have access to effective and fair services.

Communities should expand availability of supports and services designed to preserve the tribal family and culture. Active efforts are required in preventing the break-up of American Indian/Alaska Native families, which includes engaging families, and involving the child and youth, the parents, the elders, and the tribe in service delivery. A cornerstone of these efforts is involving the child and youth's tribe in decisionmaking.

Active and early participation in tribal families involved with child welfare whether on reservations and in urban communities is designed to help prevent removal and to work toward reunification. Immediate and ongoing consultation with the child's tribe is essential when supports and services are provided by entities other than the tribe. Active efforts are more intensive than "reasonable" efforts.[lxxv]

Each entity should have a mechanism for monitoring its compliance with ICWA requirements.[lxxvi]

As required by ICWA, all entities must give full faith and credit to decisions made by tribal courts concerning children who are subject to tribal jurisdiction.

CULTURALLY INFORMED AND DIVERSE

VII.4. **All entities and their staff and volunteers should be culturally informed about the diverse individuals and groups in their respective communities and among their workforce.**

People providing supports and services must recognize and respect the great diversity among children, youth, and families, and colleagues. (See also *Engagement/Participation* on page 55.)

To create organizational cultures that value diversity, respect differences, and emphasize cultural competence, providers should recruit and value having staff and volunteers that are demographically diverse, reflecting the people in the community and those receiving supports and services.

Provision of services must be culturally responsive and appropriate to the needs of children, youth, and families from diverse cultural, ethnic, religious, socioeconomic, nationalities, and other backgrounds.

IDENTITY

VII.5. **All entities, communities, and families should ensure that resources are available to help children, and youth understand their heritage, preserve their connections to culture**

and religion, learn and preserve their traditions, and have positive role models.

Families, communities, and all other entities should recognize the primacy of role models and connections to the development of strong and healthy racial, ethnic, cultural, and religious identity.

Families raising children and youth of difference races, cultures, and ethnicities must have resources available for helping them to understand those differences, and to help their children and youth to learn about, embrace, and thrive with a strong sense of who they are. They should understand the tasks involved in raising children and youth with healthy racial and ethnic identities, and should be provided with resources and tools as needed.[lxxvii][lxxviii]

INDIVIDUAL AND SYSTEMIC BIAS

VII.6. **Organizations and individuals should make commitments to becoming aware of and overcoming individual and systemic bias.** (See also *Trauma-Informed Approaches* on page 69.)

Specific strategies to overcome institutional racism and cultural bias are needed to assure that children, youth, and families are served in culturally sensitive and responsive ways. Communities and other entities should work together to recognize and reduce disparities that are a result of institutional bias. (See also the following standard.)

All staff and volunteers working with children, youth, and families should be educated about the effects of institutional and historical bias and discrimination, should be aware of the potential for bias based on implicit association,[lxxix] and should be open to changing their own attitudes and behaviors. (See also *Engagement/Participation* on page 55 and *Nondiscrimination* on page 108)

Each entity should examine outcome data for trends according to race, ethnicity, gender, and other demographic characteristics to help identify and address disparity, disproportionality, and institutional bias.

DISPARITY AND DISPROPORTIONALITY

VII. 7. **Each entity should examine disparities in its service delivery, as well as the ways in which it contributes to racial, ethnic, and other disproportionalities that negatively impact children, youth, and families.**

Everyone should understand that although neglect and abuse occur at the same rates among various communities, in many areas there are disproportional rates for reports, investigations, placement of children outside their homes, and disparities in services available, particularly among communities of color. All entities should work to correct these inequalities.

It is also essential to keep data concerning race and ethnicity of persons served so each entity may accurately track their progress toward fair and equal service availability and delivery.

YOUTH AND FAMILIES IDENTIFYING AS LGBTQ

VII. 8. **Every entity should develop expertise in understanding the unique perspectives and needs of children, youth, and adults who identify as LGBTQ.**

Estimates of youth and families identifying as LGBTQ are not exactly known; however, the U.S. Census Bureau reports statistics on same-sex married couple and unmarried partner households. According to revised estimates from the 2010 Census,[lxxx] there were 131,729 same-sex married couple households and 514,735 same-sex unmarried partner households in the United States.

Children and youth who identify as LGBTQ often face discrimination and expulsion from their homes, communities, and the programs that serve them. Each entity should include LGBTQ identity and issues among the core components of cultural competence training. Providers may develop a cohort of staff with expertise in serving this population of children, youth, and families.

Children, youth, and families that identify as LGBTQ may need specialized services and supports that do not currently exist in many communities. These children, youth, and families should be supported in advocating for development of appropriate services and supports.

IMMIGRANT CHILDREN AND FAMILIES

VII. 9. **Entities and communities should develop and implement programs that are responsive to the unique needs of families who have immigrated to the United States.**

Communities and other entities should proactively seek to identify and remove systemic bias and barriers to participation by immigrant children, youth, and families. Communities should ensure that appropriate supports and services are available without regard for visa status and/ or citizenship.

Each entity should have mechanisms for outreach to immigrant families who are concerned about seeking assistance because they fear authorities.

Communities and other entities should develop appropriate response plans and support mechanisms for children whose parents have been removed from the United States or have been denied entry.

DEVELOPMENTALLY INFORMED

VII.10. **Each entity should be well-informed about learning and developmental differences, cognitive limitations, physical and other disabilities, as well as normal growth and development.**

Entities should be well-versed in current research regarding the physical, intellectual, emotional, social, spiritual/moral development of children, youth, and families. They should understand the risk to normal development resulting from abuse, neglect, and other forms of maltreatment. The necessary knowledge base includes expected normal development as well as developmental delays.[lxxxi]

Entities must also understand and be able to work effectively with parents and other family members with developmental differences, as well as with children and youth whose parents have developmental challenges. (See also *Supports and Services* on page 67.)

When providers offer supports and services to specific populations, they should establish criteria for staff selection that ensure required minimum knowledge and skills appropriate to the group.

RESOURCES

America's Most Unwanted, a film by Shani Heckman, http://mostunwantedfilm.org/

Hardin, C. D., & Banaji, M.R. (2010). The Nature Of Implicit Prejudice: Implications For Personal And Public Policy. Retrieved from http://www.fas.harvard.edu/~mrbworks/articles/InPress_Shafir.pdf.

Green, D., Belanger, K., McRoy, R., & Bullard, L. (2011) Challenging Racial Disproportionality in Child Welfare Research, Policy and Practice. Washington, DC: CWLA Press.

Hill, R. B. (2007). An Analysis of Racial/Ethnic Disproportionality and Disparity at the National, State, and County Levels. Casey-CSSP Alliance for Racial Equity in the Child Welfare System. Retrieved from http://www.casey.org/Resources/Publications/Analysis OfDisproportionality.htm.

National Indian Child Welfare Association, 5100 SW Macadam Avenue, Suite 300, Portland, Oregon 97215. Telephone: 503-222-4044, Email: info@nicwa.org

Annie E. Casey Foundation. (2006.) *Race Matters: Unequal Opportunity within the Child Welfare System*. Baltimore, MD: Author. http://www.kidscount.org/kcnetwork/resources/RaceMattersToolkit.htm.

Srivastavaa, S. B., & Banajia, M.R. (2011). Culture, Cognition, and Collaborative Networks in Organizations. *American Sociological Review, 20*(10), 1–27.

Williams, D. *Beyond the Golden Rule: A Parent's Guide to Preventing and Responding to Prejudice*. Montgomery, AL: Teaching Tolerance. Retrieved from http://www.tolerance.org/sites/ default/files/general/beyond_golden_rule.pdf.

A "Mission Not Impossible": Understanding and Reducing Disparities and Disproportionality. Presentation by Terry Cross (2011). System of Care Community Training. Tribal and Urban Indian Systems of Care Grantee Meeting, July 18, 2011.

![CWLA]

NATIONAL BLUEPRINT

FOR EXCELLENCE IN CHILD WELFARE

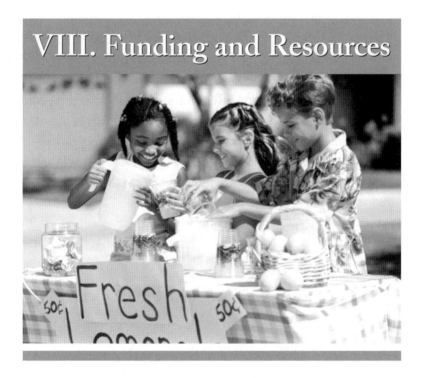

VIII. Funding and Resources

PRINCIPLE

Funding decisions in the private sector and at federal, state, local, and tribal levels are informed by the certainty that the well-being of children, families, and communities are interconnected and that sufficient and equitable funding is essential to the well-being of all of them.

In the United States, funding to support the well-being of children, families, and communities comes from tax revenues levied at all levels of government and, to a lesser extent, from private philanthropy. Pressure on all those resources coincides with demographic trends showing that a large share of children live in family circumstances that have typically hindered their access to equal opportunities.[lxxxii] [lxxxiii] [lxxxiv] It is crucial for both public and private opinion leaders to ensure the right approach to funding for children, youth, and families. While observers may differ on the right solutions, the data on children's well-being and their family circumstances suggest that results for children in the United States today do not achieve the vision that we have set forth. It is crucial for leaders to acknowledge this gap and honestly discuss their perspectives about the resources required to address it.

It is crucial for interconnectedness among the needs of children, families and communities to be at the forefront of fiscal planning, in an era when:

- states face sharp revenue constraints[lxxxv] just as family need increases;[lxxxvi]

- municipalities file for bankruptcy;[lxxxvii]

- it is the norm for funding entities to reduce budgets for supports and services for children, youth, and families;

- the fiscal health of providers is threatened by years of inadequate funding; and

- the global economy is a factor in everything from the cost of goods and services to the availability of personnel.

Government entities, whether local, state, federal, or tribal, must embrace the concept that when funding for supports and services is adequate, children, youth, and families can flourish; when funding is not adequate, they suffer. Furthermore, decreased well-being in the present is predictive of poor outcomes and increased expense in the future.[lxxxviii][lxxxix][xc] Every entity involved in funding must work toward budgeting sufficient funds for needed supports and services, eliminating waste and reducing redundancy, allocating resources wisely, and promoting a climate of cooperation rather than competition for limited dollars.

Funding should be linked to positive outcomes, and should be discontinued for programs, services, and supports that do not work or result in unintended negative consequences. To that end, funders should consider the costs of the processes and infrastructure to implement performance measures, and should provide funds to implement them.

STANDARDS

FUNDING PRIORITIES

VIII. 1. Funding decisions should be based upon the cost of effective services, the benefits such services are expected to bring, and the likely consequences (including costs) of deferring or failing to make investments in children, youth, and families. Where necessary, priority should be given to those that are most vulnerable.

Participants in funding discussions will inevitably have different perspectives and beliefs, but serious, honest, and data-based discussions of these issues are far preferable to avoiding or skirting the question of what it will take to support a shared vision for children and youth.

Too often, budget discussions with significant impact on child and youth investments occur in a limited context, with incomplete information. This can occur within one service system—for example, a state considers its child welfare budget without good information on the consequences for families of fewer child protective services workers or fewer opportunities for training. It is even more likely to occur across systems, given the interlocking context described in the National Blueprint. For example, a state may make a decision about whether to expand Medicaid under the Affordable Care Act to adults with incomes below the poverty line without taking into account the positive impact of expansion on access by parents to mental health services, which could reduce child abuse and neglect or speed reunification after entry into foster care. Greater understanding of the context and implications at all levels—whether through adoption of budgets, more effective one-on-one communication by all participating organizations, or other approaches—is a fundamental underpinning of the vision of the CWLA National Blueprint.

In addition, there must be mechanisms to measure actual costs of supports and services for children, youth, and families. Entities must be able to track outcomes related to costs, computing costs per child, per service, and per year as compared with what the costs are when supports and services are not provided. Funding entities—whether public systems, foundations, corporations, or other funders—should understand and consider the true costs of service provision and provide the funds to be able to document it.

When governments and communities invest in children, youth, and families, they are making good investments in the future.

VIII.2. Every individual, organization, and community has the responsibility to explain the impact of funding decisions,

and advocate for priority funding for supports and services for children, youth, and families.

Advocacy should focus on helping decision makers to understand that making funding for children, youth, and families a priority, and that allocating funds is the right thing to do because their well-being affects all members of society. Advocates should help decisionmakers to understand that funding prevention and early intervention services with positive outcomes in learning, health, safety, and overall well-being, is, typically, far less expensive than funding services to correct more intensive problems later on. (See also *Shared Responsibility and Leadership* on page 41.)

VIII. 3. Funders should collaborate with each other, with communities, and with providers to identify needs and shared priorities, promote sensible application and eligibility criteria, identify obstacles, and allocate funds and other resources wisely.

Collaboration to provide everything needed for children, youth, and families to flourish is a shared responsibility that extends to funders of all types. (See also *Shared Responsibility and Leadership* on page 42 and *Collaboration* on page 41.) Funders, whether they are foundations, corporate giving programs, other grant makers, or government/public funders, have an obligation to work together to address the needs of children, youth, and families and the providers that work with them.

Funders should consider conducting assessments of needs and assets together, issuing joint requests for proposals, coordinating application dates, and pooling resources. Funders should find ways to combine their training and technical assistance resources, convene multiple grantees for shared learning opportunities, and share the lessons learned from their grantees. Funders should collaborate to improve the efficiency and effectiveness of seeking and awarding funds.

FUNDING IMPLEMENTATION OF THE NATIONAL BLUEPRINT

VIII. 4. Funders should promote and fund concepts and strategies that are consistent with the CWLA National Blueprint's vision, values, principles, and standards.

Funders should become familiar with the CWLA National Blueprint, and should use the document to guide funding priorities, the scope and content of requests for proposals, letters of intent, grant applicants, and contracts and agreements.

VIII. 5. Funders should support evidence-based and evidence-informed programs and practices. (See also *Quality Improvement* on page 86, and *Evidence-Based* and *Evidence-Informed* on page 16.)

The proliferation of evidence-based and evidence-informed programs and practices depends upon adequate funding to support them. Costs associated with purchasing materials and implementing programs and practices supported by solid evidence can be higher than those associated with practices less well-researched and documented. Funders should be willing to invest in programs and practices that can demonstrate efficacy and positive outcomes.

VIII. 6. Funding sources should provide financial assistance to build evidence of efficacy of promising practices.

Funders should recognize that most practices that eventually become evidence-based were at some point "promising practices." Funders should consider that costs associated with accumulating evidence of efficacy of new and promising practices can be substantial, and should be willing to fund research and other evidence-building. (See also *Research* on page 90.)

VIII. 7. Public entities and other funders should provide financial incentives to support organizations' efforts to employ and engage people with experience as a service recipient. (See also *Experience as a Service Recipient* on page 97 and *Shared Responsibility and Leadership* on page 38.)

Youth and family involvement should be more than superficial. There should be paid positions that bring family, youth, and former clients into the work. (See also *Workforce* on page 96 and *Engagement/Participation* on page 50.)

Governmental grants and contracts should include contingencies for family involvement, and funding applicants that have sound plans for meaningful engagement of youth and families with experience as a service recipient should be prioritized for funding over other applicants.

FUNDING EQUITY

VIII. 8. Funding for supports and service should be equitable.

There should be equitable levels of funding across urban and rural environments.

Funding sources should be mindful that matching fund requirements can be prohibitive for poor jurisdictions and can effectively eliminate them from competition for certain grants and funding opportunities.

There should be funding equity across jurisdictions. American Indian and Alaska Native supports and services should not be funded less because tribal governments administer them.

PUBLIC-PRIVATE COLLABORATION

VIII. 9. Entities with contractual and funding relationships should work together to be jointly accountable and to ensure that funding for supports and services for children, youth, and families is adequate, equitable, and that there is the wisest possible use of public and private funds.

There should be a true public-private partnership to share the risks, rewards, and responsibilities of delivering services to children and families. To the extent allowed by procurement rules, a collaborative public-private planning process can ensure that consensus is reached, that fiscal accountability is shared equally, and that collaborative and cost-saving strategies can be identified.

In many jurisdictions, privatization or partial privatization of human services has become the norm.[xci] Privatizing a child welfare service does not relieve the public child welfare agency of its responsibilities to ensure that children and families are well served and that tax dollars are effectively spent. Meanwhile, a private organizational recipient of public funding has an obligation to manage funds well and be accountable for them.

In addition to the quality improvement program components identified in the *Quality Improvement* section of the National Blueprint, public entities should develop quality assurance systems that systematically review contract performance and hold funded recipients accountable,[xcii] while enabling them to manage the services they are enlisted to provide.

DIVERSE FUNDING STREAMS

VIII. 10. Organizations should seek diverse funding streams to produce income from contracts, grants, investments, corporate and foundational giving, and individual donations.

Providers should not be totally reliant upon funding from any single source. Diversity of funding streams helps entities to maintain fiscal health, and to manage reallocation of funding when fiscal challenges are encountered.

Funders, especially contracting authorities, should commit to providing adequate funding for the programs and services being purchased under contract. Grants and contracts should not prohibit augmentation of funding through fundraising or other subsidy when the funds provided by the grant or contract are insufficient for the program at hand.

ACCOUNTABILITY AND TRANSPARENCY

VIII. 11. **Funders, contractors, donors, and the general public should have access to accurate accounting of funds for supports and services for children youth and families.**

Whether public or private, nonprofit or for-profit, each entity should have accurate budgets and accounting records that are available for review. Entities should expect and be entitled to funding only when they are accountable for the funds that they receive.

SOCIAL ENTERPRISE

VIII. 12. **Business, philanthropic, venture capital, and public and private nonprofit entities should work together to harness the power of social enterprise.**

Social enterprises are businesses whose primary purpose is the common good. They use the methods and disciplines of business and the power of the marketplace to advance their social, environmental and human justice agendas.

Social enterprises are distinguished from other businesses, nonprofits, and government entities by three essential characteristics:

- They directly address a social need through the goods and services they provide, or by employing people who are considered disadvantaged;

- They have a commercial activity that produces significant income; and

- The good accomplished by the social enterprise is a primary purpose for its existence.

Social enterprises were for many years a component of nonprofits that used business models and earned income strategies to pursue their mission. Current social enterprises include both for-profit and nonprofit entities, and are a social mission. Social enterprises have been identified as a creative solution to the challenge of providing employment to people who are unemployed or underemployed. At the same time, public officials often support the concept of social sources of revenue for entities that are underfunded.

Governments, communities, corporations, and small businesses should work together with nonprofits to identify opportunities for social enterprise development and expansion.

RESOURCES

Casey Family Programs. (2010). *Ensuring Safe, Nurturing and Permanent Families for Children: The Need to Reauthorize and Expand Title IV-E Waivers.* Retrieved from http://www. casey.org/resources/publications/pdf/NeedForWaivers.pdf.

Casey Family Programs.(2011). *Ensuring Safe, Nurturing and Permanent Families for Children: The Role of Accountability in Child Welfare Finance Reform.* Retrieved from http://www.casey.org/Resources/Publications/pdf/AccountabilityPaper.pdf.

APHSA Gainful Employment and Independence: A Pathways Policy Brief—August 24, 2012, http://www.aphsa.org/Policy/OC1.asp

V. Kasturi Rangan, Leonard, H. B., & McDonald, S. (2008). *The Future of Social Enterprise.* Harvard Business School Working Paper.

Shapiro, R. A. (2013). *The Real Problem Solvers: Social Entrepreneurs in America.* Stanford, CA: Stanford Business Books.

REFERENCES

I. RIGHTS OF CHILDREN

[i] American Academy of Pediatrics. Healthy Children.org. (2011). Gender identity and gender confusion in children. Retrieved from http://www.healthychildren. org/English/ages-stages/gradeschool/Pages/Gender-Identity-and-Gender-Confusion-In-Children.aspx.

[ii] U.S. Department of Education, National Center for Education Statistics. *Condition of Education 2010; 2011; 2012.* Retrieved from http://nces.ed.gov/pubsearch/.

[iii] Committee on Pediatric Workforce, American Academy of Pediatrics. (1993). Reaffirmed Policy Statement: Pediatric Primary Health Care. Pediatrics, 127(2), 397. Retrieved from http://pediatrics.aappublications.org/content/127/2/397.full.

[iv] Gershoff, E.T. (2008). *Report on Physical Punishment in the United States: What Research Tells Us About Its Effects on Children.* Columbus, OH: Center for Effective Discipline.

[v] American Academy of Pediatrics, Committee on Psychosocial Aspects of Child and Family Health. (1998). Guidance for Effective Discipline. *Pediatrics, 101*(4), 723–728.

[vi] American Psychoanalytic Association. *Position Statement Regarding Physical Punishment.* Retrieved from http://apsa.org/About_APsaA/ Position_Statements/ Physical_Punishment.aspx.

II. SHARED RESPONSIBILITY AND LEADERSHIP

[vii] Kouzes, J.M., & Posner, B.Z. (2007) *The Leadership Challenge, 4th Edition* (pp. 208-209). Hoboken: John Wiley & Sons, Inc.

[viii] Kretzmann, J.P., & McKnight, J.L., (1993) Building Communities from the Inside Out: A Path Toward Finding and Mobilizing a Community's Assets. (p.6). Retrieved from www.oac.state.oh.us/.../BuildingCommunitiesEnglish/ BuildingComm.

[ix] Kobasa, S. C. (1979). Stressful life events, personality, and health – Inquiry into hardiness. *Journal of Personality and Social Psychology, 37*(1): 1–11.

[x] Bartone, P. T., & Hystad, S. W. (2010). Increasing mental hardiness for stress resilience in operational settings. In P. T. Bartone, B. H. Johnsen, J. Eid, J. M. Violanti & J. C. Laberg (Eds.), *Enhancing human performance in security operations: International and law enforcement perspective* (pp. 257–272). Springfield, IL: Charles C. Thomas.

[xi] Ibid.

[xii] Sid Gardner (2007). *Time After Time: Reflections on Forty-plus Years of Collaboration and Service Integration*. White Paper. Stewards of Change. Retrieved from http://www.stewardsofchange.com/LearningCenter/Documents/WHITE_PAPERS/Time%20After%20Time.pdf.

[xiii] Entwistle, T., & Martin, S. (2005). From competition to collaboration in public service delivery: A new agenda for research. *Public Administration, 83*(1), 233–242.

[xiv] Pecora, P.J., Cherin, D., Bruce, E., & Arguello, T. (2010). *Administrative supervision: A brief guide for managing social service organizations (Chapter 1)*. Newbury Park: Sage Publications.

III. ENGAGEMENT/PARTICIPATION

[xv] Perry, B. D., Beauchaine, T. P., & Hinshaw, S. P. (2008). Child maltreatment: a neurodevelopmental perspective on the role of trauma and neglect in psychopathology. In T.P. Beauchaine & S.P. Hinshaw (Eds.), *Child and adolescent psychopathology* (pp. 93 –221). Hoboken, NJ: John C. Wiley & Sons, Inc.

[xvi] Perry, B.D. The neurodevelopmental impact of violence in childhood. (2001). In D. Schetky & E.P. Benedek (Eds.), *Textbook of Child and Adolescent Forensic Psychiatry.* (pp. 221–238). Washington, DC: American Psychiatric Press, Inc.

[xvii] Clark,H.W., &. Power, A.K. (2005). Women, Co-occurring Disorders, and Violence Study: A case for trauma-informed care. *Journal of Substance Abuse Treatment, 28*(2), 145–146.

[xviii] McHugo, G.J., Kammerer, N., Jackson, E.W., Markoff, L.S., Gatz, M., Larson, M.J., Mazelis, R., & Hennigan, K. (2005). Women, Co-occurring Disorders, and Violence Study: Evaluation design and study population. *Journal of Substance Abuse Treatment, 28*(2), 91–107.

[xix] Center for Family Finding and Youth Connectedness. Retrieved from http://www.senecacenter.org/perm_resources.

[xx] Wilson, K. R., & Prior, M. R. (2011). Father involvement and child well-being. *Journal of Paediatrics and Child Health, 47*(7),405–407.

[xxi] Villanueva, C., & Byrne, M. W. (2009). *Mothers, Infants and Imprisonment A National Look at Prison Nurseries and Community-Based Alternatives.* New York: Women's Prison Association, Institute on Women and Criminal Justice.

IV. SUPPORTS AND SERVICES

xxii American Academy of Pediatrics. (2012). Policy Statement: Pesticide Exposure in Children. *Pediatrics, 130*(6), e1757–e1763. Retrieved from http://pediatrics. aappublications.org/content/130/6/e1757.

xxiii Sawhill, I.V., Winship, S., and Grannis, K.S. (2012). *Pathways to the Middle Class: Balancing Personal and Public Responsibilities.* Center for Children and Families, Social Genome Project, Brookings Institute. Retrieved from http://www.brookings. edu/~/media/research/files/papers/2012/9/20%20 pathways%20middle%20 class%20sawhill%20winship/0920%20pathways%20middle%20class%20sawhill %20winship.

xxiv YMCA. Linking Policy And Environmental Strategies To Health Outcomes. Retrieved from http://www.ymca.net/healthier-communities-guide.

xxv Brennan Ramirez, L.K,. Baker E.A., & Metzler M. (2008). *Promoting Health Equity: A Resource to Help Communities Address Social Determinants of Health.* Atlanta: U.S. Department of Health and Human Services, Centers for Disease Control and Prevention. Retrieved from http://www.cdc.gov/nccdphp/ dach/chhep/pdf/ SDOHworkbook.pdf.

xxvi Thomson, G., et al. (2006). Population level policy options for increasing the prevalence of smokefree homes. *Journal of Epidemiology and Community Health, 60*(4), 298–304.

xxvii National Council on Disability. *Rocking the Cradle: Ensuring the Rights of Parents with Disabilities and Their Children.* (2012). Washington, DC: Author.

xxviii Lietz, C.A. (2006). Uncovering Stories of Family Resilience: A Mixed Methods Study of Resilient Families, Part 1. *Families in Society, 87*(4), 586–582.

xxix Kawachi, I., & Berkman, L.F. (2001). Social ties and mental health. *Journal of Urban Health, 78*(3), 458–467.

xxx Coleman-Jensen, A. , Nord, M. Andrews, M. and Carlson, S. (2012) *Household Food Security in the United States in 2011.* ERR-141, U.S. Department of Agriculture, Economic Research Service. Retrieved from http://www.ers.usda.gov/media/ 884525/err141.pdf.

xxxi Weinreb, L. Wehler, C. Perloff, J. Scott, R. Hosmer, Sagor, L. and Gunderson, C. (2002) Hunger: Its Impact on Children's Health and Mental Health. *Pediatrics, 110*(4), e41.

xxxii Generations United. *Hunger and Nutrition in America: What's at Stake for Children, Families and Older Adults.* (2012). Washington, DC: Author. Retrieved from http://www.gu.org/LinkClick.aspx?fileticket=5VYHjMiKL 9U%3D&tabid=157&mid=606.

xxxiii Centers for Disease Control. Adverse Childhood Experiences (ACE) Study Outcomes. Washington, DC: Author. Retrieved from http:// www.cdc.gov/ace/ outcomes.htm.

xxxiv National Center for Medical Home Implementation. Retrieved from http://www. medicalhomeinfo.org/.

xxxv The American Academy of Pediatrics. (2002) The Medical Home. *Pediatrics, 110*(1), 184–186.

xxxvi Felitti, V.J., et al. (1998). Relationship of Childhood Abuse and Household Dysfunction to Many of the Leading Causes of Death in Adults: The Adverse Childhood Experiences (ACE) Study. *American Journal of Preventive Medicine, 14*(4), 245–258.

xxxvii U.S. Department of Health & Human Services. Health Information Accountability and Portability Act (HIPAA). Washington, DC: Author. Retrieved from http://www.hhs.gov/ocr/privacy/hipaa/administrative/statute/hipaastatutepdf.pdf.

xxxviii Health Information Technology for Economic and Clinical Health (HITECH) Act. Retrieved March 26, 2013, from https://www.federalregister.gov/articles/2010/07/28/2010-17207/medicare-and-medicaid-programs-electronic-health-record-incentive-program.

xxxix U.S. Department of Health & Human Services. (2012). Affordable Care Act. Retrieved from http://www.health care.gov/law/full/index.html.

xl Pakenham, K. I. (2009). Children who care for their parents: the impact of disability on young lives. In C.A. Marshall , E. Kendall , M. Banks, & R.M.S. Gover, (Eds.), *Disability: Insights From Across Fields and Around the World, Vol II,* (pp. 39–60). Westport, CT : Praeger Press.

xli American Association of Caregiving Youth. See http://www.aacy.org/.

xlii Cohen, D., Greene, J.A., Toyinbo, P.A., & Siskowski, C.T. (2012). Impact of Family Caregiving by Youth on Their Psychological Well-Being: A Latent Trait Analysis. *The Journal of Behavioral Health Services and Research, 39*(3), 245–256.

xliii Diaz, N., Siskowski, C. & Connors, L. (2007). Latino Young Caregivers in the United States: Who are they and what are the Academic Implications of this Role? *Child Youth Care Forum, 36,* 131–140.

xliv Barquet, Nelson (2011). The Internet and Social Media: A Curse On Our Kids? Not If They Are Caregiving Kids. Retrieved March 26, 2013, from http://ezinearticles.com/?The-Internet-and-Social-Media:-A-Curse-On-Our-Kids?-Not-If-They-Are-Caregiving-Kids&id=6148090.

xlv   Centers for Disease Control. Adverse Childhood Experiences (ACE) Study Outcomes. Washington, DC: Author. Retrieved from http://www.cdc.gov/ace/outcomes.htm.

xlvi   Weinberger, A.H., McKee S.A., & Mazure, C.M. (2010). Inclusion of women and gender-specific analyses in randomized clinical trials of treatments for depression. *Journal of Women's Health 19*(9), 1727–1732.

xlvii Brumbaugh, S. and, J. Hardison Walters, and L. Winterfield. (2010) *Suitability of Assessment Instruments for Delinquent Girls.* U.S. Department of Justice Office of Justice Programs, Office of Juvenile Justice and Delinquency Prevention. Retrieved from https://www.ncjrs.gov/pdffiles1/ojjdp/ 226531.pdf.

xlviii Thomas, C. (2009). Gender and Juvenile Justice: New Courts, Programs Address Needs of Girls. *Youth Law News, 28*(3). Retrieved from http://www.youthlaw.org/publications/yln/2009/july_september_2009/gender_and_juvenile_justice_new_courts_programs_address_needs_of_girls/.

xlix   National Center for State Courts. Performance Measurement Resource Guide. Retrieved from http://www.ncsc.org/Topics/Court-Management/Performance-Measurement/Resource-Guide.aspx.

l   Chang, J.O. (2012). Social Media Use in Child Welfare. *Children's Bureau Express, 13*(11).

li   Oshima, N., et al. (2012). The Suicidal Feelings, Self-Injury, and Mobile Phone Use After Lights Out in Adolescents. *Journal of Pediatric Psychology 37*(9): 1023–1030.

lii   Schmidt, M.E., Pempek, T. A., Kirkorian, H.L., Lund, A.F., & Anderson, D. R. (2008). The effects of background television on the toy play behavior of very young children. *Child Development, 79*(4), 1137–1151.

liii   Bowman, L. L., et al. (2010). Can students really multitask? An experimental study of instant messaging while reading. *Computers & Education, 54*(4), 927-931.

liv   Ybarra, M. L., Mitchell, K. J., Hamburger, M., Diener-West, M., & Leaf, P. J. (2011). X-rated material and perpetration of sexually aggressive behavior among children and adolescents: Is there a link? *Aggressive Behavior, 37*(1), 1–18.

lv   Lenhart, A.. Digital Divides and Bridges: Technology Use Among Youth, Pew Internet & American Life Project, Pew Research Center. Annenberg Presentation, April 13, 2012. Retrieved from http://pewinternet.org/Reports/2012/Digital- differences.aspx.

lvi   Ibid.

lvii   Federal Trade Commission. The Children's Online Privacy Protection Act (COPPA). Retrieved from http://www.business.ftc.gov/privacy-and-security/children's-privacy.

V. QUALITY IMPROVEMENT

[lviii] California Evidence-Based Clearinghouse. What is Evidence-Based Practice? Retrieved from http://www.cebc4cw.org/what-is-evidence-based-practice/.

[lix] California Evidence-Based Clearinghouse. Retrieved from http://www.cachildwelfareclearing house.org.

[lx] ChildTrends Flourishing Children Project. Retrieved from http://www.child-trends.org/_docdisp_page.cfm?LID=0D4A5339-82B7-4F9A-87334D04E D13E922#FCP.

[lxi] Evidence Based Practice or Practice Based Evidence: Is It One or the Other? Children's Bureau, Centennial Topical Webinar Series, July 17, 2012. Retrieved from https://cb100.acf.hhs.gov/downloads/E-BPorP-BE_ PPT.pdf.

[lxii] Moore, K.A. & Lippman, L. H. (Eds.). (2005) *What Do Children Need to Flourish? Conceptualizing and Measuring Indicators of Positive Development.* Berlin: Springer Science+Business Media.

VI. WORKFORCE

[lxiii] CPS HR Consulting. (2007). The RJP Tool Kit: A How-To Guide for Developing a Realistic Job Preview. Retrieved from http://www.cps.ca. gov/workforceplanning/documents/ToolKitRJP.pdf.

[lxiv] Glisson, C., & Green, P. (2011). Organizational climate, services, and outcomes in child welfare systems. *Child Abuse and Neglect, 35*(8), 582–591.

[lxv] Pecora, P.J., Cherin, D., Bruce, E., & Arguello, T. (2010). *Administrative supervision: A brief guide for managing social service organizations.* Newbury Park: Sage Publications.

[lxvi] Coaching In Child Welfare. Child Welfare Matters, Summer 2012. Retrieved from http://muskie.usm.maine.edu/helpkids/rcpdfs/cwmatters12.pdf.

[lxvii] Bride, B. Secondary Trauma and the Child Welfare Workforce, PowerPoint Presentation, presented May 1, 2012, at The 13th Annual CASCW Conference: Beyond Burnout: Secondary Trauma and the Child Welfare Workforce. Retrieved from http://www.cehd.umn.edu/ssw/cascw/ events/SecondaryTrauma/PDFs/BrianBride_PPT.pdf.

VII. RACE, ETHNICITY, AND CULTURE

[lviii] Tervalon, M. & Murray-García, J. (1998). Cultural Humility Versus Cultural Competence: A Critical Distinction in Defining Physician Training Outcomes in Multicultural Education. *Journal of Health Care for the Poor and Underserved, 9*(2), 117–125.

lxix Title VII of the Civil Rights Act of 1964 (Pub. L. 88-352) (Title VII). Retrieved from http://www.eeoc.gov/laws/statutes/titlevii.cfm.

lxx ADA 2010 Revised Requirements. U.S. Department of Justice Civil Rights Division, Disability Rights Section. Retrieved from http://www.ada.gov/revised_effective_ dates-2010.pdf.

lxxi The U.S. Equal Employment Opportunity Commission. Questions and Answers, Retrieved from http://www.eeoc.gov/facts/qanda.html.

lxxii MA 102 CMR 3.04(3)(l.) "The licensee may not discriminate in providing services to children and their families on the basis of race, religion, ethnic background, cultural heritage, national origin, marital status, sexual orientation or disability, or in approving shelter home parent applicants on the basis of age, sex, race, religion, ethnic background, cultural heritage, national origin, marital status, sexual orientation or disability." Retrieved from http://www.mass.gov/edu/docs/eec/regs-policies/residential-regs.pdf.

lxxiii Blackstock, C., Cross, T., George, J., Brown, I, & Formsma, J. (2006). *Reconciliation in child welfare: Touchstones of hope for Indigenous children, youth, and families.* Ottawa: First Nations Child & Family Caring Society of Canada and Portland, OR: National Indian Child Welfare Association. Retrieved from http://www.reconciliationmovement.org.

lxxiv Ibid.

lxxv National Indian Child Welfare Association. *The Indian Child Welfare Act: A Family's Guide.* Portland, OR: Author. Retrieved from http://www.nicwa. org/Indian_Child_Welfare_Act/documents/FamilysGuidetoICWA2012.pdf.

lxxvi Indian Child Welfare Act United States, Code Title 25, Chapter 21. Retrieved from http://www.nicwa.org/policy/law/icwa/icwa.pdf.

lxxvii Crumbley, J. (1999). Seven Tasks for Parents: Developing Positive Racial Identity. Adoptive Families. Retrieved from http://www.nacac.org/postadopt/transracial_identity.html.

lxxviii Raible, J. (2008). The significance of racial identity in transracially adopted young adults. In *Transracial Parenting in Foster Care and Adoption: Strengthening Your Bicultural Family.* Ankeny, IA: Iowa Foster & Adoptive Parents Association.

lxxviii Project Implicit, Harvard University. Retrieved from https://www.projectimplicit.net/index.html.

lxxx Retrieved from http://www.census.gov/newsroom/releases/archives/2010_census/cb11-cn181.html.

lxxxi Center for Advanced Studies in Child Welfare. (2012). Using a Developmental Approach in Child Welfare Practice. *SW360º*, Winter 2012.

VIII. FUNDING AND RESOURCES

lxxxii Issacs, J., Toran, K., Hahn, H., Fortuny, K., Stueerle, C.E., Kids Share 2012. Urban Institute Report on Federal Expenditures on Children Through 2011. Retrieved from http://www.urban.org/UploadedPDF/412600-Kids-Share-2012.pdf.

lxxxiii ibid

lxxxiv For example, in 2011, about 22% of children lived below the federal poverty line and about the same share in struggling families just over the poverty line (below twice the poverty line).

lxxxv U.S. Department of Commerce, U.S. Census Bureau U.S. Census Bureau Reports State Government Revenues Decline Nearly 31 Percent. Retrieved from http://www.census.gov/newsroom/releases/archives/governments/cb11-03.html.

lxxxvi Brandon, R., Povich, D. & Mather, M. (2012) *Low-income working families: the growing economic gap.* Working Poor Families Project. Retrieved from http://www.workingpoorfamilies.org/wp-content/uploads/2013/01/Winter-2012_2013-WPFP-Data-Brief.pdf.

lxxxvii See http://www.governing.com/gov-data/municipal-cities-counties-bankruptcies-and-defaults.html.

lxxxviii Shi Y., Sears, L.E., Coberley, C.R., & Pope, J.E. (2012). Classification of individual well-being scores for the determination of adverse health and productivity outcomes in employee populations. *Population Health Management,* September 26, 2012.

lxxxix Harrison P.L., Pope, J.E., Coberley, C.R., & Rula E.Y. Evaluation of the relationship between individual well-being and future health care utilization and cost. *Population Health Management, 15*(6), 325–330.

xc Pew Center on the States, Partnership for America's Economic Success (2011). *Paying later: the high costs of failing to invest in young children.* Retrieved from http://www.readynation.org/uploads/20110124_02311PAES CrimeBriefweb3.pdf

xci McBeath, B., Collins-Camargo, C., & Chuang, E. The Role of the Private Sector in Child Welfare: Historical Reflections and a Contemporary Snapshot Based on the National Survey of Private Child and Family Serving Agencies. *Journal of Public Child Welfare, 6*(4), 459–481.

xcii U.S. Department of Health and Human Services, Office of the Assistant Secretary for Planning and Evaluation. (2008) *Ensuring Quality in Contracted Child Welfare Services.* Washington, DC: Author.

INDEX

A

B

C

D

S

T

U

V

W